The ALGEBRA
o*f* **SALES** αnd
PERSUASION

blazer *sales*

"What makes this book stand out is how Brad simplifies the often confusing world of persuasion. He combines research with practical advice, making this book a valuable read for anyone looking to improve their sales skills."

Dave Elsner
The Tech Sales Coach

"This book reads like a personal chat and training session. Brad shares stores from his decades of experience and valuable concepts that he developed in the trenches. There are a lot of sales books, but nothing like this!"

Travis Isaacson, Founder
Powder Days Marketing

"Such a genius book! Brad's insights helped me uncover a blindspot in my sales approach. This is a must read for anyone involved in complex product or services selling."

Kip Meacham, Director of Business Development,
VPI Technology

"I highly recommend The Algebra of Sales and Persuasion to anyone in sales or sales leadership as a tool to up your game, skyrocket your effectiveness, and make more meaningful impressions on prospects and clients. I enjoyed the anecdotes from Brad's globetrotting sales adventures."

Michelle L. Page, Founder
RevenueChasers LLC

"The Algebra of Sales and Persuasion, is a great read providing fantastic perspective for all sales pro's. It's a definite must read for people looking to up their game and be better for themselves and their clients."

Dionne Mejer, Founder and CEO, Revenue By Design
Author of *The Stepped Approach*

ISBN 979-8-9906968-0-8   *paperback*

ISBN 979-8-9906968-1-5   *ebook*

ISBN 979-8-9906968-2-2   *audiobook*

The Algebra of Sales and Persuasion

Proven formulas, strategies, and stories from a globetrotting sales executive

braddavidball.com

blazer *sales*

The **ALGEBRΔ** o*f* **SALES** α**nd** PERSUASIΦN

Proven formulas,
strategies, and stories
from a globetrotting
sales executive ✈

BRAD DAVID BALL

*"**A shoe is just a shoe until someone steps into it.** Then it has meaning."*

Contents

Introduction. 1

1   The Buyer's Journey 9

2   Persuasion. 27

3   Sales Algebra. 37

4   Crafting a Sales Narrative 47

5   How to Build Credibility 65

6   Microstories. 109

7   Emotional Selling 133

8   Slide Deck Strategies. 145

9   Delivering Your Presentation 161

10 Closing the Deal 173

11 The Get vs. Go Framework 183

Conclusion 201

Notes 205

Expanded Contents 209

Acknowledgements 215

About the Author. 217

Let's Connect. 219

Free Resources 221

Introduction

Singapore is an impressive country. Located just above the equator on the tip of the Malay Peninsula, it's long been a strategically important location for international trade. Today, it's home to the world's second-largest port, and it's a thriving business hub bolstered by attractive tax laws and an abundance of talent from both the East and West.

If there's a big conference or expo in Southeast Asia, it's often held in Singapore. And if it's in Singapore, the Marina Bay Sands is often the destination of choice. Owned and operated by the Las Vegas Sands Corp., the expo center is located adjacent to the world-famous Marina Bay Sands Hotel (the one with the epic infinity pool on the top) and one of the most luxurious shopping malls in the world.

Over the years, I've attended many events at the Marina Bay Sands. I've also heard and delivered many sales presentations in that expo hall. However, one incident from a conference a few years ago stands out. Perhaps nobody remembers it (but me)—and that's just the point: nobody remembers!

At this particular conference, there was an educational session with about two hundred guests ready to hear a panel of speakers. I happened to be one of the four panelists and was in my seat on the stage as the session began at 10:00 a.m. sharp. The meeting host soon approached the lectern to welcome the attendees and go over a few items of business. He then briefly introduced the sponsor of the event and welcomed to the stage a well-dressed European gentleman who I recognized as the owner of the sponsoring business.

Stop for just a moment to think about this opportunity from a sales perspective.

This business owner paid thousands of dollars to sponsor this event and deliver an eight- to ten-minute sales pitch in front of hundreds of potential clients.

Before him was an audience of decision-makers within his industry, many of whom needed his product and had considerable discretion over their budget.

For the next few minutes, he had their undivided attention. What an extraordinary opportunity!

Unfortunately, this opportunity went largely wasted. His sales pitch was flat, his message irrelevant, and his slide deck chock-full of entirely forgettable information.

Three minutes in, I looked around the room to observe the audience. Most were unengaged, looking at their phone or flipping through the conference program.

I found this situation truly fascinating. Here was this polished, highly educated business owner who had paid handsomely for the opportunity to deliver a sales presentation in front of a target rich audience. He had traveled halfway around the world to deliver his pitch, yet it was mediocre in almost every way. At the end of the eight minutes, the audience gave him a courtesy applause, he walked off stage, and the conference continued.

I'm almost certain this businessman has no idea he did a mediocre job. If you were to ask him (immediately afterward) how things went, I'm confident he would have responded positively. But if you were to poll any audience member, I'm sure the vast majority would have already forgotten the details of his presentation.

Watching this situation up close, from the unique perspective of being on the stage looking down at the audience and their reaction during the presentation, opened my eyes somewhat.

In the years since, I've watched as similar circumstances have played out at other conferences I have attended throughout the world. From Atlanta to Rotterdam, from Ho Chi Minh City to New York City, I've witnessed sophisticated and capable professionals deliver surprisingly unremarkable—or just plain terrible—sales presentations to audiences everywhere.

Most sales presentations aren't delivered to a large audience in a conference hall—many are delivered in boardrooms, dining rooms, and showrooms; some on doorsteps; and others over the phone or via Zoom.

All too often these presentations are structured wrong— they include or focus on the wrong information at the wrong moment.

Just as a powerful boxer is not effective in the ring if his timing is wrong and his combination punches never land—an otherwise skilled presenter will miss out on a lot of opportunities if their message and timing are not structured correctly.

There's a huge opportunity cost to delivering a mediocre sales presentation. It happens far too frequently—usually by sales professionals and business owners who have a plethora of talent and skills but have never been taught the right techniques.

So what makes a compelling sales pitch? Why are so many sales presentations bland? If given the opportunity to deliver a high-stakes sales presentation, how do you make sure it doesn't bomb?

As it turns out, there is a formula that, if followed, can turn a bland sales pitch into one that's effective and persuasive.

But there's much more to selling than just delivering a great presentation. Sales professionals must learn how and when to engage with the buyer, ask the right discovery questions, understand their pains and needs, and communicate a powerful value proposition. Perhaps most of all, sellers need to get the buyer emotionally involved. This can be easier said than done. Where does one start?

Over the course of my career, I've been the recipient of a massive amount of sales education. I've learned from some of the best and received instruction at the undergraduate, graduate, and executive levels. Like many others, I've participated in many corporate sales trainings and read countless sales books. Truthfully, there's a lot of good content written and taught about in the world of sales.

However, in my view, there's a misalignment in virtually every bit of sales training I've ever received. There are some core principles that are rarely if ever taught to most sales professionals—it's somewhat baffling to me.

To this day, some sales education focuses on closing tactics and techniques. I view this type of sales training with great skepticism.

Other content focuses on prospecting and strategies designed to add more prospects to the top of the funnel. I find this material interesting and useful, but somewhat limited when considering the entire sales cycle.

There's also a great amount of content, methodologies, and sales training that deals specifically with asking the right questions during the discovery process. I greatly value and learn from this type of content and even touch on some of it in this book—but not all methods will be applicable in every industry.

Early in this book I introduce a couple of concepts that are well known in disciplines adjacent to sales, but not taught directly in most sales courses and curriculums. One is a principle popular among marketing and communication experts, but glossed over among most B2B sales professionals. Another framework I introduce is used by debate teams, lawyers, and politicians to convince and persuade, but rarely is it top of mind to professional sellers.

In the first few chapters, I take these concepts and build a workable sales framework. It's a big-picture approach to selling that, much like the branch of arithmetic from which this book is named, includes principles and fundamentals that are core and common to all.

Just as with mathematics, if you know how to set up a problem, if you know the order of operations, you can get much closer to solving for X.

Yes, sales cycles, processes, and techniques can vary drastically from retail to medical, software to advertising, and more. But while this book is written for and mostly applicable to the world of B2B sales, the ideas and fundamentals should resonate with anyone looking to elevate their ability to sell and persuade.

Whether you're preparing to deliver a sales presentation to a large group in Singapore (or elsewhere), pitching over the phone, following up with a lead via email, preparing a lengthy proposal for an RFP, managing a sales pipeline, or strategizing with a global sales team, I firmly believe the frameworks and strategies shared in this book, what I call "SALES ALGEBRA," will change and clarify your perspective on sales and magnify your sales performance.

CHAPTER 1

The Buyer's Journey

Technology and Sales Organizations

During my first year of college in the mid-1990s, I took an entry-level computer class. It was a required course taught in a lab on Tuesdays and Thursdays. I remember a big part of the curriculum was learning DOS (Disk Operating System) and the BASIC computer language. The course wasn't particularly interesting to me—but I did well and received an excellent grade.

Years later, after transferring to another university and progressing toward my degree, I received a call from my college counselor. He informed me of a problem with my transcript. Apparently the credits from that entry-level computer course taken back in 1995 would not count toward graduation. I would need to retake the same course if I wanted to stay on track. I reluctantly re-enrolled, hoping to breeze through the curriculum and quickly earn the necessary credits.

Literally nothing was the same the second time I took the class in 1999. There were no command prompts to memorize, no BASIC computer language to learn. The world had changed, and the new curriculum was focused on MS Office, email, and the Internet. Instead of learning BASIC, the entire class learned Microsoft Excel, Access, and basic HTML.

The technology leap from 1995 to 1999 was significant, as people started connecting to the Internet for the first time to explore, research, and more. A decade later there was another technological leap that occurred from around 2007 to 2010. The world went from flip phones to smartphones while simultaneously adopting social media during that era.

Few would argue—the technology boom over the last thirty years has made our daily lives exponentially easier in many ways. Amazon, Google, Netflix, and Meta (Facebook), along with hundreds of other companies that weren't even around a generation ago, have both created and capitalized on technology advancements. Our lives are now more connected and arguably more convenient by magnitudes compared to when I attended college in the 1990s.

Yet for all the perks technology brings us, there are some drawbacks. One minor example that's often cited is the disappearance of cursive handwriting—which is no longer being taught in many schools or used in daily life. Ultimately, the poor penmanship of our younger generations may not be too relevant in the grand scheme of things. However, other changes may be more significant and controversial. As a parent of teenagers, I (along with many others) have concerns about the long-term mental health impacts on our youth, who spend hours each day consuming games and social media on small screens. In many cases, the true long-term impact of our obsession with content viewed on our smartphones is not fully understood. Also complicating the matter, technology is forward-facing—the cat is essentially "out of the bag" with some of these issues. The world is not going back to an era without smartphones or the Internet. We must play with the hand we've been dealt. This is but one controversial example—there are countless others.

If we zoom in from the broad view of society and focus more specifically on the world of business, we see all sorts of examples of new technologies and innovations over the past few decades. We also see that in many cases, these technologies and innovations often have side effects and/or unintended consequences associated with them. Amazon.com has been one of the great business success stories of the new millennium. Most of us enjoy the incredible convenience of shopping on Amazon.com and would hesitate to give it up. However, it's also easy to recognize that Amazon's success and popularity have dealt an incredible blow to the broader retail industry over the last couple of decades. How many of us have gone to a shopping mall where we've seen and touched an item, only to go home and purchase the exact same product online? Guilty.

Now let's zoom in one more time from the broader business world to look specifically at how technology has impacted the world of B2B sales. As an experiment, take a journey with me back to the 1990s.

Let's look at CRM (customer relationship management) systems and compare and contrast the CRM systems we use today to those from before the turn of the century.[1] CRM systems from that era were cumbersome and had terrible user interfaces. They were also server based, not cloud based, meaning the data resided on a local area network and was not accessible to anyone outside of the office. Of course, that didn't really matter because smartphones hadn't been invented yet and even technologies such as Wi-Fi wouldn't become mainstream for several more years.

In the late 1990s, many small and mid-sized companies (and even some large organizations) used off-the-shelf CRM software. Products such as ACT or Goldmine were popular well into the 2000s. These "one-size-fits-all" applications made it difficult (or impossible) to customize fields and workflows. It may seem hard to believe, but in many cases, the IT guy (not the sales manager) was in charge of setting up, syncing, and, in some cases, managing the CRM system. Sales professionals and even some sales managers would ignore or avoid using the company CRM system altogether—until it was forced upon them by senior management. Many relied on spreadsheets, daily planners, or task lists that synced to their email software or electronic handheld device (aka PalmPilot). Most sales offices I can remember had a whiteboard that closely tracked metrics and was updated frequently by the sales manager.

While technologies such as the common spreadsheet may seem like a woefully obsolete way to manage correspondence by today's standards, it was still light-years ahead of the era just prior (1970s—1980s) when sales reps relied on 3x5 cards, notepads, file folders, and a Rolodex to keep track of everything.

Yet even in these prior eras, with sloppy processes and simple technology, the world survived—things were bought and sold, and big deals were closed. I personally worked with one well- respected sales leader who stuck with the same methods and technology as the world around him changed. He did most of his communication over the phone and refused to use the company CRM all the way until his retirement in the early 2010s.

Here in the 2020s, we live in the golden age of CRM systems. In minutes you can sign up online and build out your own custom cloud-based CRM with any process and workflow you can dream up. Salesforce.com was the first bellwether company to offer this type of SaaS product. Now, companies such as HubSpot, Zoho, Pipedrive, and many others allow companies to build out their entire sales process online.

Even some small companies today have sophisticated sales processes that are configured and managed directly by a sales leader (not the IT guy). Emails, tasks, notes, proposals, and more are all in one place and accessible anywhere via secure login from desktop, laptop, or mobile device.

Unintended Consequences of Fancy CRMs

If technology has created different challenges and unintended consequences in the world of business and society in general, could the same be true with our modern CRMs and over-engineered sales processes? I would argue YES.

First, let's clear the air. I'm not suggesting CRMs are bad for sales organizations or that we should revert to a time before we lived and breathed sales processes. Quite the opposite—studies show that over 91 percent of organizations with over eleven employees use a CRM system, and organizations that adopt a CRM are considerably more productive than those without.[2]

Virtually every sales professional who's had a legitimate B2B sales job in recent years has had to learn a CRM system. Most organizations begin training a new hire on the CRM as part of their onboarding plan. Usually, the ink isn't even dry on a new hire's offer of acceptance before they're given a password to the CRM and taught about the sales processes and various stages of the sales cycle.

Too often a sales leader will overengineer the sales process when configuring the CRM. They'll chop up the sales cycle into bite-sized pieces (sales stages) and link these stages to various percentages.

A typical sales funnel may end up looking something like this:

Sales Stage	% Chance of Closing
1- Prospecting	5%
2- Qualification	15%
3- Proposal	40%
4- Follow up	75%
5- Negotiations	90%
6- Deal closed	100%

There's a problem though: this is NOT typically how the buyer sees the situation.

Sales processes and pipeline percentages are all seams and stitching created by the sales manager. Whereas the buyer doesn't care about seams and stitching—they're not looking at the product from the inside-out view. The Buyer's Journey is different—their perspective is often simpler. Buyers typically don't care about your quota or a follow-up call, discovery meeting, or proposal review so you (as the seller) can move the opportunity along in the funnel before quarter end. Their needs are different.

There are surely unintended consequences of using a sophisticated CRM. For all the advantages that CRMs provide, too many sales professionals and sales leaders adhere so strictly to complex (and sometimes misguided) sales processes and rules that they've developed a blind spot when it comes to recognizing and understanding the Buyer's Journey.

Remember my old-school colleague who refused to use the company CRM until he retired? Yes, his methods were antiquated, and he may have ruffled a few feathers by refusing to use the company CRM. Turns out he was also a brilliant salesperson specializing in large multi-million-dollar military contracts with the US Army and US Navy. He understood the intricacies of an extremely complicated Buyer's Journey and was well respected. Ultimately, his deep knowledge of the Buyer's Journey earned him many millions of dollars over the course of his career.

For today's B2B sellers, it may be possible to have your cake and eat it too. Modern CRMs can help manage our correspondence and enhance our productivity like never before. If we couple today's technological advantages with a true knowledge and understanding of the Buyer's Journey—and learn how to interact and influence buyers as they progress toward a decision—our potential for success can skyrocket.

The Buyer's Journey ARC

The Buyer's Journey isn't just a core principle; it's a critical building block to understanding sales and persuasion. Understanding and knowing the Buyer's Journey is like understanding and knowing addition and subtraction. It's necessary to fully grasp the concept before you can move on to solving the other elements of a more complicated equation. Also, much like addition and subtraction, it's easy to learn and apply.

Before going any further, let's define and explain the Buyer's Journey in detail.

In short, the Buyer's Journey is the stages (or phases) the buyer goes through before making a purchase. In its most simple form, the Buyer's Journey has three phases: awareness, research, and choice. Think of them as a simple acronym (ARC), and visualize an arc that moves upward, ending at the top (with a purchase).

BUYERS JOURNEY A.R.C.

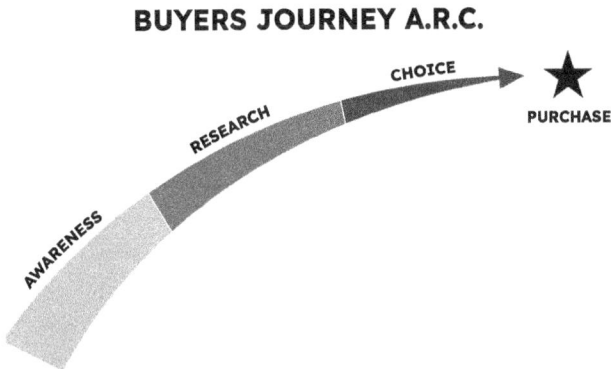

CHOICE

RESEARCH

AWARENESS

PURCHASE

Awareness Phase

There's a very simple way to determine if a potential buyer is in the awareness phase—they will tell you! Anyone or any company or organization that's in the awareness phase will immediately inform you, "We're not in the market" for whatever you're selling. In most industries, and in most cases, the vast majority of the population is in the awareness phase. (It may be as high as 99 percent.) This doesn't mean they're not curious. It also doesn't mean they're not aware of you or your company.

The range here is pretty vast. At the bottom end of the spectrum, you have someone who may have never even heard of you, your company, or your product—they may even be unaware of any sort of problem or need.

At the top of the awareness phase, you may have someone who may know a considerable amount about the products and services you offer. For simplicity's sake, think of the automotive industry. In the general public, there are many people who are passionate about automobiles. They may be fans of a particular make or model and know every detail, every specification, and even the options associated with the vehicle. The defining factor with regard to where they are in the Buyer's Journey is not their product knowledge, it's their situation. If asked, the vast majority of people (despite many of them having a significant amount of product knowledge about automobiles) will tell you they're not currently in the market—they are in the AWARENESS phase of the Buyer's Journey.

Research Phase

In the research phase of the Buyer's Journey, the prospective buyer "is" in the market—and generally they will inform you if asked. Usually there's been a catalyst—something has happened and pushed them from the awareness phase to the research phase.

Possible catalysts:

- Organization won a grant and has money for a new product

- Individual got a bonus and is ready to make a purchase

- Company leadership approved a budget

- New boss is motivated to make a change

- Something is broken and needs to be fixed

- Contract with an incumbent provider has expired

- Advertisements have motivated a proactive buyer

As we'll show later in this book, your actions and communications should be different when dealing with someone in the research phase. Typically, there's a thirst for information when a buyer enters this phase. Good sellers know how to quench that thirst.

Choice Phase

The choice phase is the final step in the Buyer's Journey. A decision is imminent and expected. The prospective buyer feels as if they've done their due diligence, and they're now ready to make a decision. They're compiling all knowledge and research and conducting final deliberations. In many cases they're evaluating quantifiable data and discussing the intangibles (i.e., gut feel) before making a final purchasing decision.

In some B2B industries, the choice phase is where you'll find a formal RFP (request for proposal)—also known as a *tendering* process. Typically, when a large company or government entity wants to make a significant purchase, they will issue an RFP and invite bidders to submit a formal response. Most of the time, this invitation will have instructions, a due date, and specific requirements to which the seller must adhere. Depending on the industry, RFPs are extremely common and often take a considerable amount of time and attention from sales professionals (and sometimes from an entire team). The key thing to understand about RFPs is they almost always come after the buyer has done a considerable amount of research. A company soliciting an RFP is most likely in (or approaching) the choice phase of the Buyer's Journey. If you're a seller and just being introduced to a company or a specific opportunity via RFP, you may be a little bit late to the party. Generally speaking, the earlier you (as a salesperson) are introduced to the buyer in the journey, the better chance you have of influencing a decision and ultimately winning the deal.

Mapping the Buyer's Journey

To better understand the Buyer's Journey ARC, it's useful to run through some common examples. As the tenets of the Buyer's Journey are universal, you can easily map one out for almost any legitimate sales transaction.

Start by mapping out the Buyer's Journey for a common consumer purchase as these types of transactions are simple. Once you get some practice, try a more complex sale.

As you're mapping out these Buyer's Journey examples, take note of two additional items:

1. The catalyst: The event or action that propelled the buyer to move from the awareness phase to the research phase.

2. The first encounter: The first instance the buyer is likely to encounter a salesperson.

Mapping the Buyer's Journey—including the catalyst and the salesperson's first encounter—helps us to view the Buyer's Journey from the buyer's perspective. There are many advantages to learning and understanding buying triggers that will help us to strategize our approach.[3] Ultimately, this will impact the way we communicate and interact with prospective clients.

Buyers Journey **ARC**

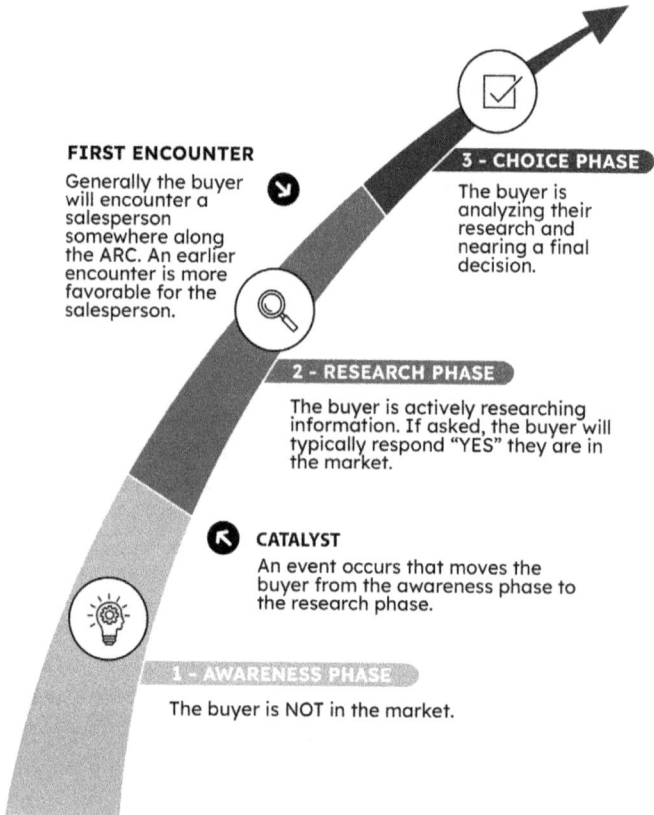

FIRST ENCOUNTER

Generally the buyer will encounter a salesperson somewhere along the ARC. An earlier encounter is more favorable for the salesperson.

3 - CHOICE PHASE

The buyer is analyzing their research and nearing a final decision.

2 - RESEARCH PHASE

The buyer is actively researching information. If asked, the buyer will typically respond "YES" they are in the market.

CATALYST

An event occurs that moves the buyer from the awareness phase to the research phase.

1 - AWARENESS PHASE

The buyer is NOT in the market.

Just by going through a few examples, you should be able to easily walk up to a whiteboard and scratch out a Buyer's Journey ARC. With a little practice, you'll quickly be able to do this for just about every imaginable situation. It's possible to drill down deep into each phase, defining (for instance) the amount of awareness a typical buyer will have before the catalyst pushes them into the research stage. It's certainly helpful to understand these phaseses in depth for your given industry and company. However, it's not necessary to overcomplicate—just be able to quickly think about and identify where a potential buyer is in their journey.

Now that you understand the Buyer's Journey, you understand the first part of the equation that makes up Sales Algebra. The real magic happens later, when we pair the Buyer's Journey with some additional knowledge. Yet if this book were to conclude right here, there's still some enormous value to understanding the Buyer's Journey in and of itself. The Buyer's Journey gives us perspective and pulls us out of the "CRM" mode. Rather than look at a sales process simply as a matter of stages within the CRM, we can look at opportunities more objectively, which can spur new ideas and help us get deals unstuck. Additionally, as sellers, we can gain perspective and more accurately forecast when an opportunity might close.

CHAPTER 2

Persuasion

A Brief History of Persuasion

Do you know someone who is truly persuasive? When that word comes to mind, who do you think about? It may be a skilled politician. In American politics, there's no shortage of persuasive political leaders and pundits. John F. Kennedy and Ronald Reagan were both superb communicators who knew how to persuade. In today's era, there are countless politicians and pundits at the local and national levels who are gifted in the science of persuasion.

You don't necessarily need to look at politics. Your local high school probably has a debate team with some teenagers who are very capable of making a persuasive argument. I still recall a young woman from my high school years who starred on the debate team. She was quite the orator and had an impressive ability to persuade others to her side of an argument—even if the question was as simple as new wave versus rock music.

The core concepts of persuasion are not a mystery, and persuasive tactics didn't just arise in the twentieth century—the core elements have been known for at least two millennia. Aristotle is generally credited as the father of persuasion. Yes, the same Aristotle (Ancient Greece philosopher) that you probably learned about in tenth grade.

Aristotle taught about ethos, logos, and pathos. These are likely not words or concepts you're hearing for the first time. However, as you'll soon find out, we're going to take these centuries-old methods and use them in a new context.

Ethos, Logos, Pathos

It is worth a quick review of ethos, logos, and pathos to refresh the concepts in our minds before we add some fuel to the fire. For those who are already rolling their eyes and getting weary at the thought of rehashing ancient Greek philosophy—take solace—the refresher will be brief, and I can assure you, we will soon move on to more interesting and entertaining territory.

Ethos: In the context of persuasion, *ethos* means "credibility." It's an appeal to trustworthiness. It's the reason why advertisers like to use doctors to promote medicine, and athletes to promote sporting goods and shoes. The perception (real or not) is that these experts and celebrities are credible resources and know a thing or two about the product.

A lot of things can lend to credibility, including experience, formal education (degrees), longevity, knowledge, perceived expertise, and more. Ultimately, it comes down to trust—does the buyer (or person being persuaded) trust the seller? Without ethos, selling becomes a very difficult proposition.

Logos: *Logos* is "logic." It's the numbers, the statistics, the proof. It's the stuff engineers and accountants absolutely love. It's also incredibly boring and over-emphasized by inexperienced sales professionals everywhere. There's a place for logos in selling—it's a necessary ingredient, much the same way salt is a key ingredient in a cookie. But it must be used sparingly and delivered correctly.

Pathos: The simple definition for *pathos* is "emotion." This is perhaps the most effective and powerful way to advertise and sell. Humans make purchasing decisions based on their emotions. On a consumer level, this happens multiple times per day without us even realizing it. The global consumer advertising business (a US$700 billion industry) has a heyday creating persuasive advertisements that inspire us to take micro-actions that result in the subtle *beep* of an Apple (or Android) payment. Recently, at the movie theater, just before the previews started, there was a short video showing a cup of soda being filled to the brim. The accompanying audio featured the undeniable fizz of a cold fountain drink. It was a short twenty-second ad—but incredibly effective. Less than two minutes later, I had a cold drink in my hands and was rushing back to my seat before the feature film started. This is classic pathos—appealing to the raw senses (in my case, thirst and the feeling of satisfaction). Sold!

Beyond consumer advertising, pathos is still a mightily effective method in B2B selling. It surely begins with good marketing—highlighting features on a website, in a brochure, via videos, etc. Once a sales professional is involved, pathos is often delivered via a story. An effective communicator can craft an analogy or story that highlights a product, answers a question, and delivers a dose of emotion along the way. In many cases, the product can be seen, touched, or otherwise experimented with. While the emotion may not be delivered quite as directly as the sugar rush of a cold fountain drink—a prospective buyer in the B2B space that's allowed to experiment and test a product may be able to envision themselves (or their organization) as happy and satisfied users. This is an effective use of pathos in selling.

Can you spot the ethos, pathos, and logos? Politicians, debaters, and marketers are always using ethos, pathos, and logos to their advantage. If you want to see these on display, just visit YouTube and do a quick search for "persuasive commercials," where you'll find enough examples to take up the rest of your afternoon.

Powerful Examples of Ethos, Logos, Pathos

Not surprisingly, most commercials made for TV feature heavy doses of pathos. With such limited time, many thirty- to sixty-second advertisements are trying to impact (or even manipulate) your emotions through some sort of sadness, nostalgia, excitement, humor, or satisfaction. Usually this is delivered through the telling of a brief story.

An emotional advertisement from Chevrolet a number of years ago showed a young woman in her early twenties with her ailing dog. In sixty seconds, the advertisement shows flashbacks in reverse chronological order. We watch a girl with the dog at her side as she goes to college, breaks up with a boyfriend, learns to drive, and celebrates a birthday. Ultimately, we see her as a young girl picking up the dog as a puppy. The Chevy SUV (of course) plays a supporting role in many of the scenes. During the entire sixty seconds, a melancholy piano is playing, helping to create the crescendo of emotion. Finally, in the last few seconds, a script appears: "A best friend for life's journey." Powerful pathos!

Perhaps some of the most influential advertisements in the history of TV are those that feature ethos, logos, and pathos working together. While this may be a rare phenomenon during a short commercial, it happens every day on QVC and the Home Shopping Network. If you're shaking your head right now, perhaps you know someone who has a compulsion to purchase products from one of these channels. The truth is, they're extraordinarily persuasive because they make use of ethos, logos, and pathos during each segment. However, there is one flaw: viewers immediately know they're being pitched. There's an ethos (credibility) deficit up front that causes the vast majority of television viewers who stumble upon a shopping network to immediately change channels. But for those who stay, perhaps intrigued by the product being presented at that moment, they're in for a polished presentation featuring heavy doses of ethos, logos, and pathos.

One of the most legendary infomercial pitchmen in television history was Billy Mays. In the 1990s and 2000s he promoted a series of products. He had a certain style, a shtick—he spoke fast and often shouted at the camera. This style became a bit of annoyance for many, who upon hearing his voice would instantly lose appeal and change the channel. So how was he so successful in his heyday?

The true reason for Billy May's success was his effective use of ethos, logos, and pathos in a short one- to two-minute window of time. Many of Billy May's commercials can now be seen on YouTube. A quick search led me to one of his early advertisements for a popular product (still on the market) called OxiClean. During this advertisement, Billy delivers a concentrated dose of ethos, logos, and pathos. As he aggressively talks at the camera, delivering facts (logos) about OxiClean, he is simultaneously providing a demonstration (pathos) of the solution as the product effortlessly removes red wine from the carpet. Occasionally, some ethos is thrown into the mix, usually delivered with the line, "We've sold millions," which helps him establish credibility for any viewer that may be tuning in. Even as someone fully aware of the tactics he was using, I was a bit mesmerized by the effectiveness and persuasiveness of this advertisement created over two decades ago. I honestly thought to myself for a moment, "Wow—maybe I need to pick up some OxiClean!"

For us, the real question is, how do we properly use some of these persuasive tactics in our own situation? Yes, advertisers and marketers use ethos, logos, and pathos, but can these concepts be converted and used by entrepreneurs and sales professionals? If so, how and when do we use these tactics in an effective manner? In the next chapter we'll explore and demonstrate exactly how and when to use these methods to great effectiveness—without all the shouting and the 1-800 numbers used by Billy Mays and his peers.

CHAPTER 3

Sales Algebra

Back in chapter 1, we became familiar with a simple version of the Buyer's Journey ARC. In chapter 2, we reviewed the core concepts of persuasion as taught by Aristotle. By themselves, these concepts are useful, but certainly not groundbreaking from any perspective. However, when we marry these principles, some clarity and enlightenment result. I like to refer to this as Sales Algebra.

The parallel or analogy with algebra is simple—when learning the basic concepts of algebra and solving for "X," one must learn to pay attention to both sides of an equation. In this case, the Buyer's Journey ARC is one side of the equation, and Aristotle's core concepts of persuasion are the other side of the equation. They are very much linked together. Let's take a closer look.

The Best Strategy for the Awareness Phase

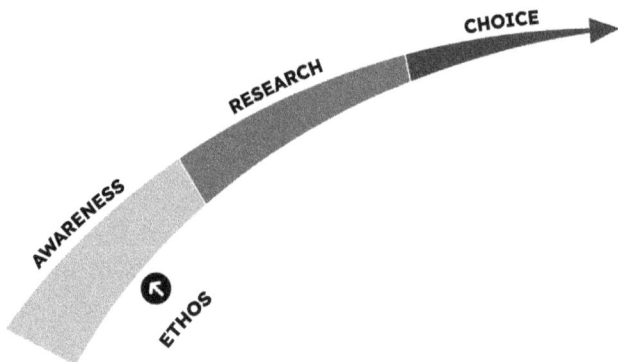

Think of someone in the awareness phase of the Buyer's Journey. Remember, they're not in the market for what you're selling. They may be familiar with your company or product, but if asked, they will clearly inform you they're "not looking."

When trying to sell to someone in this early phase of the Buyer's Journey, it can be difficult to move the needle. What works? Detailed statistics? Evidence showing the usefulness of your product? How about a passionate customer testimonial?

No. It's not the time to use emotion.

If you're trying to appeal to a prospective customer by delivering a story or testimonial, it won't work. Offers to demonstrate a product will most likely fall on deaf ears.

In the early phase of the Buyer's Journey, forget about persuading. What you need to focus on is ethos or (more specifically) building credibility. Your goal as a professional salesperson is to make a positive and favorable impression. Credibility and competence are the impression you're trying to make. In some cases, your entire objective during this phase of the Buyer's Journey is simply to get on the buyer's radar—plant a seed—and nothing more.

In this early phase of the Buyer's Journey, credibility always wins, and your actions and dialogue should concentrate on how you can build credibility and trust with the buyer. Be especially aware of introducing pathos (emotion) into the awareness phase, as you can quickly lose credibility by coming across as too salesy.

It is far too common among B2B sellers to be pitching, persuading, and selling while a prospective buyer is in the awareness phase. The salesy-ness this can create in most situations (whether B2B, retail, phone sales, door-to-door, or any other type of sales environment) can be cringe-worthy. I often refer to this as the "original sin of selling." The original sin—acting salesy—is literally the exact opposite of the approach that should be used to build credibility.

The Best Strategy for the Research Phase

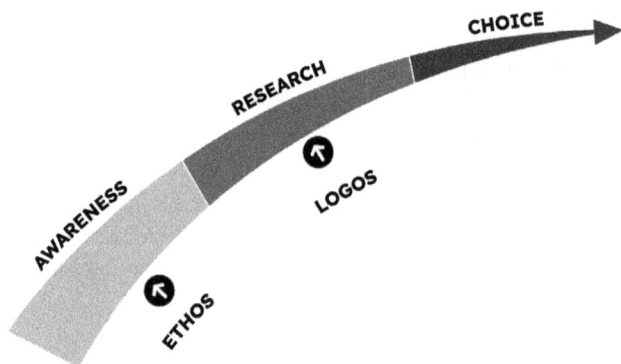

Moving up the ARC of the Buyer's Journey, past the awareness phase, we have the research phase of the Buyer's Journey. As you recall, this is the point when the buyer is actively looking for a solution, investigating and researching different options. In most cases, the buyer will be open about the fact they are in the market for a new product or service.

In this phase, the buyer is thirsty for information—so we provide them exactly what they're looking for: logos, or specifically the logic, facts, numbers, statistics, and evidence.

While logos can effectively be used anywhere in the Buyer's Journey, a buyer in the research phase will be more interested and receptive to details and specifics than a buyer in the awareness phase.

A word of caution—logos must be used somewhat sparingly. It's too often overused and abused. Overdosing on logos can result in buyer boredom and the loss of a personal connection with the buyer.

Keep in mind that usually, inbound leads, whether from a referral, trade show, or website inquiry, are in the research phase of the Buyer's Journey. As a salesperson, if you're given an inbound lead, understand that the person with whom you're communicating desires detailed information, specs, price, etc.

Your best strategy is to act quickly to supply the buyer with some of the information they desire and create a dialogue. Data dumping all the specs, pricing, and details is not the best approach. It may also be too early for an emotional pitch. (That comes later.) However, strategically supplying the buyer with information and sussing out their motivations, desires, and pain points is typically the right move.

The Best Strategy for the Choice Phase

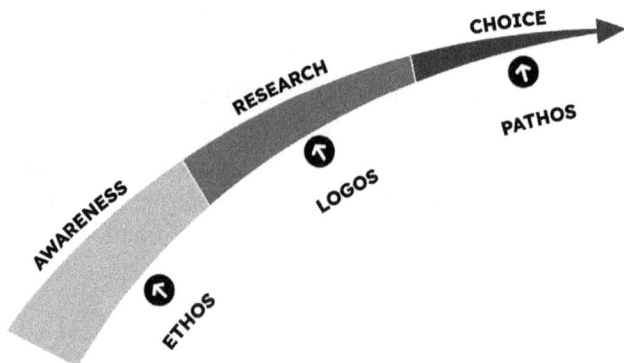

The final phase of the Buyer's Journey is where we pull out all the stops. The buyer is now keenly aware of the product or service; they've received and compiled information. A decision is becoming imminent.

When someone reaches this phase, we can inject pathos into the equation. We want the buyer to have an emotional connection with the product or service. This is where we, the sellers, can use stories and testimonials or (in many instances) create an emotional connection by letting the buyer experiment with the product.

In some cases, there is a hard indicator when the buyer moves from the research phase to the choice phase of the Buyer's Journey—a formal RFP is such an event. However, in many cases, particularly with more transactional and less expensive items, the Buyer's Journey can quickly move from the research phase to the decision phase. As a seller, it is key to determine when, how, and how much pathos to inject into your approach.

Order of Operations

There's a certain inherent truth when we merge the Buyer's Journey with Aristotle's methods of persuasion. These are psychologically linked together in virtually all selling situations and can be scaled or consolidated as necessary to always construct a compelling sales pitch, so long as they're kept in the proper order.

Always start with credibility (ethos).

Then add evidence and logic (logos).

Finally, end with an emotional appeal (pathos).

Whether discussing these as part of the greater Buyer's Journey (which may take weeks, months, or years depending upon your industry), an hour-long presentation given to an audience, or even a one-on-one sales pitch delivered over the telephone in three minutes, these will always construct a salient sales pitch when delivered in the correct order. Consider this the overhand knot of sales messaging. Once you grasp this core concept, it becomes possible to craft a sales pitch and create sales messaging in almost any situation.

Experts on persuasion suggest the three modes of persuasion should not necessarily be thought of in a linear way but more like three overlapping circles (as long as they are all present).[4] This may be sufficient when delivering a speech or writing an essay; however, in a sales situation, the order is perhaps more important because credibility must be established first and throughout the pitch. Logos and pathos follow later.

CHAPTER 4

Crafting a Sales Narrative

Now that we've introduced the Buyer's Journey, discussed the core concepts of persuasion, and married them together in a framework called Sales Algebra—let's look at some examples, practical strategies, and tactics that can help sales professionals in their daily work. I've found in my own career that some of the best learning happens when I make mistakes.

Misdiagnosing a Prospective Buyer

Many years ago I was on an extended sales trip in China. This was before the trade wars and political tension between the USA and China escalated in the 2010s.

After several meetings in the Shanghai area, I had a final sales meeting in a place called Qinhuangdao. This is a city in Northeastern China, best known as the location where the Great Wall meets the ocean. It's also home to one of the largest coal ports in the world.

I arrived in the city with my local representative (who also acted as my translator) and spent the evening before my meeting doing some sightseeing. The next morning, we headed off to our prescheduled appointment with a large company that had expressed interest in purchasing a training simulator for a mining reclaimer system.

As we approached the corporate office, I noticed my name on a large electronic sign—but I didn't think much of it at the time. Then when we arrived, I saw that my name was again displayed, this time on the marquee in front of the main building: "Welcome, Mr. Brad Ball."

As I entered the lobby, a large contingency was there to greet me personally. The CEO, along with several executives and engineers, was present. A small press corps was on hand to take a few pictures and document my visit. I was treated like an ambassador—yet in the back of my mind, I was wondering, "Why all the hoopla for a brief introductory meeting?"

A few minutes later I learned that this was not an introductory meeting. The company had already done their due diligence and completed an extensive amount of research. I was not made aware of this beforehand.

I was only three slides into my presentation, and the engineers were already asking highly technical questions. The expectation was for me to answer these questions so we could then finalize other terms and conditions during my visit. The entourage was there believing they were going to witness the signing of a major deal.

Meanwhile, my presentation included some very basic information—it would have worked just fine if they had just heard about my company and our technology for the first time. That was not the case. They had detailed and specific questions relating to their situation—I had no answers. I did my best to bluff my way through the meeting, but in the end, even the language barrier provided little to no cover for the awkward humiliation.

In short, this company was clearly in the final stages of the research phase of the Buyer's Journey. They needed me to answer a few technical questions before they made a final decision. My introductory presentation had assumed they were in the awareness phase. The meeting was not only an embarrassment but also caused an immediate loss of credibility for both me and my company. The opportunity with this prospective client was lost.

This is a somewhat unique example. Very often, the exact opposite scenario that I've just described is true. A salesperson will deliver a presentation with all sorts of specifications and facts. In some cases, they'll even give an in-depth product tour explaining features and spewing details. Meanwhile, the buyer is still in the awareness phase. The presentation comes across as uninspiring or boring. If you recall, this is the exact situation I observed in Singapore that I described in the opening introduction to this book.

Misdiagnosing where your prospective buyer is in their journey can send your deal off track quickly. At the very least, it can also lead you down the wrong path, crafting an irrelevant or ineffective message at an inopportune time. The result will be a boring, inconsequential sales pitch. Yes, the audience may give you a courtesy clap. Your host or point of contact may thank you for coming—but the excitement and interest level will be lackluster. Worse yet, you may lose credibility and become fodder for some good laughs after you leave (as I'm sure happened in my case after I left Qinhuangdao).

Steps to Crafting an Effective Sales Pitch

How can we take what we've learned about the Buyer's Journey ARC and the methods of persuasion to craft an effective sales pitch?

Here's where to start . . .

The first step in the process is to simply identify who is in the audience. Who will be hearing your pitch?

Once we've identified the audience, let's quickly sketch out an ARC to identify where they're at in the Buyer's Journey.

Now that we know where they are in the Buyer's Journey, we can quickly match it to the appropriate method of persuasion.

Are you giving an introductory presentation to a potential buyer in the awareness phase? Focus your content on building ethos (credibility).

Presenting to someone in the research phase? Be prepared with stats, facts, and evidence (logos) to help present your case.

Are you pitching to an informed buyer—someone or some company that has been researching your product for some time? Chances are they're in the choice phase of the Buyer's Journey, meaning you should use pathos in your presentation. Use emotion, customer testimonials, and (if possible) a demonstration to create an emotional connection between the buyer and your product or service.

In some instances, you may be speaking to a larger audience, perhaps at a conference or event in front of dozens of different people. In this case, simply ask the questions, "Who is the average audience member in attendance? Where are they in the Buyer's Journey?" Make your best educated guess to answer these questions, and then match the appropriate method of persuasion and build your presentation accordingly.

What to Include in Your Presentation

Your presentation should never focus solely on one specific method of persuasion. Your pitch should include all three modes of persuasion on some level. Even if you've identified that your audience is in a specific phase of the journey (i.e., the research phase) you can't go into your presentation with only numbers and statistics. It will still be necessary to establish some credibility (ethos) and deliver some sort of emotion (pathos).

The same goes if you're delivering your presentation to an audience that is in the awareness phase of the journey. In most cases, when delivering a presentation or speech to a large group, the audience will be in the awareness phase, and your presentation should primarily focus on building credibility. However, you can't completely neglect the logos or pathos. You will need to have at least some evidence and emotion to share in your pitch.

The simple analogy here is to imagine you have three cars in your garage. Each represents the type of sales pitch you can deliver. The first is a sports car, the next is an SUV, and the last is a sedan.

All three are capable vehicles. All three can get you from point A to point B. Which should you take?

The Sports Car

The sports car represents pathos and emotion. It's the most thrilling—biggest—upside. It's also a bit risky. What if it rains? What if there's a bumpy gravel road? It's best to be somewhat cautious when taking out the sports car. First, make sure the prospective buyer is at (or at least near) the *choice* phase of the Buyer's Journey.

When might you want to use the sports car? It's usually OK when you're among friends and the weather is clear.

There are also some rare opportunities that you'll pull it out as a last-ditch effort when in danger of losing a deal. Sometimes as a salesperson you intuitively know you're in trouble. Perhaps you're not the preferred vendor, or perhaps the prospect has expressed doubts along the way and this could be your last opportunity.

The strategy here (if it's a long-shot deal) is to take a risk. Pull out the sports car, take down the top, rev the engine, and deliver your best pitch with an emotional appeal. The sports car gives you the highest upside: there's a chance you can inspire the buyer and win the deal. It's also very possible that you'll come across as "salesy" and you may risk embarrassment. But if you've got nothing to lose, this could be your best play. Why not?

The SUV

The SUV in this analogy represents logos or evidence. The SUV can manage bumpy gravel roads and inclement weather. No, it's not particularly fast or fun to drive, but it's durable and reliable—it gets the job done.

Are you delivering a pitch to a group that's in the research phase of the Buyer's Journey? They're thirsty for information; they're seeking statistics, evidence, and specifications. Perhaps there are engineers or accountants in the group who will be pushing to know all the details. If this is the case, your sales pitch better contain more than just a few emotional stories. Come prepared with the SUV, loaded up with some evidence and statistics that will appeal to your audience.

The Sedan

The sedan may be the most important vehicle in your garage because it typically works well in most situations. The vast majority of the time, you're not looking to race up a mountain road to impress a passenger or go off-roading. As with most sales presentations, most of the time your audience will be in the awareness phase of the Buyer's Journey. This is particularly true if you are pitching to a larger audience at a conference or event. They're not looking for in-depth stats or evidence. They don't need to hear a detailed customer testimonial or see a demonstration. What you need to showcase is your credibility.

The sedan I use as a daily driver is a BWM. It has all-wheel drive and a twin-turbo engine. It tries to be all of the above (a sedan, a sports car, and an SUV), and it does a pretty decent job. If there's inclement weather or a bumpy gravel road, the AWD manages pretty well unless the conditions are extreme. No, it doesn't have the clearance or superb traction of an SUV, but in most cases, it does well. My BMW even has a little button that allows me to select the mode I desire. When I'm occasionally on a curvy mountain road or want to impress a passenger, I can select Sport Mode while I roll down the windows, open the sunroof, and turn up the music. No, it isn't as thrilling as a true sports car, but the twin-turbo can certainly impress if needed.

To be an impactful seller, you should construct your sales pitch like a performance sedan. As a default, we should seek to build credibility. However, as needed, we should have the ability to handle like a SUV, effectively presenting statistics and evidence as necessary. Then, at the click of a button, we should be able morph into a sports car, delivering an exciting and emotional appeal that has the ability to impress and deliver impact.

Opportunity + Solution + Benefits Framework

If you're in doubt about where to start, there's a very simple framework that can help. This framework, when used properly, allows you (the seller) to not only structure a simple sales presentation, but also to build credibility, introduce evidence, and sell with emotion. You can effectively cover all of your bases (ethos, logos, pathos) using this approach. Aristotle would be proud!

The best thing about this framework is that it's scalable, meaning it works when building a pitch deck but also works brilliantly in short sales conversations.

Even beyond selling, this same framework can be used to persuade and influence others to great effect. Skilled debaters use variations of this framework all the time when structuring their arguments and crafting responses.

Here's how it works . . .

Introduce a Opportunity

First, introduce an opportunity. There are generally two kinds of opportunities you can present:

1- Economic opportunity which will help the buyer save (or make) money. Typically these opportunities are framed around ROI (return on investment).

2- The opportunity to solve a specific problem or pain.

In many cases, these are intertwined and you can introduce an opportunity that will not only solve a problem, but help a buyer financially.

Your goal is to build up credibility by showing that you know and understand the customer's situation and industry.

Often the way to go about introducing this opportunity is to frame it inside a challenge or problem that a potential customer is facing. This could be something broad or very specific.

A good way to begin is stating something similar to the following:

"What I've found throughout your industry is _____ challenge. Has your organization experienced this same issue?"

Present a Solution

Now that we've introduced an opportunity (and likely discussed a challenge or problem the prospective customer is facing), we can't just leave it hanging. Even if we've drilled down into the consequences and specific details, there comes a time when we must present our solution.

Ideally, your solution is straightforward and easy to comprehend. The product, service, or idea that you present should be the perfect solution to the opportunity you've just described. It's important that your solution makes sense—it must have a logical appeal.

Share Benefits (Give an example)

Next we present the benefits of our product/service. We share relevant stories and customer testimonials. In some cases we may provide an example or demonstration. The goal is to bring some emotion into the mix.

You may have identified a pattern. The Opportunity + Solution + Benefits Framework is a simple variation of ethos, logos, pathos.

Consider...

By introducing an opportunity—hopefully we exhibit some knowledge about the situation and build credibility (ethos).

Next, we present a solution—logical in nature that has laid out how our product/service is the anecdote to a problem. Doing this typically requires sharing some details and specifications (logos).

Finally, by sharing impactful stories and providing a demonstration or example, we evoke a little bit of emotion (pathos).

Selling to Someone with No Pain or Problems?

When creating a pitch deck and developing your sales narrative, there's a tendancy to focus on the problems and pain. It's low hanging fruit. A skilled salesman might be able to quickly uncover the pain, present a solution, get the prospective customer excited through a demonstration, and have them ready to sign.

Often, it's not quite that easy.

There are instances where you may be selling to someone or an organization that isn't struggling. Things are going well, and there's no real "pain" or problems to solve.

A former colleague of mine once sold luxury vessels (yachts). This is not an industry where buyers are suffering or feeling an exorbitant amount of pain.

Beyond the luxury market, there's also missionary selling—introducing a new product to a market where clients have never purchased before.

In this case, a seller is likely to hear things such as, "Why fix what isn't broken?" or, "We've never needed this before."

Some sales trainers suggest digging deeper to find pain that the buyer may not even realize is there. However, this may be the wrong approach.

Instead, a salesperson should try to frame the situation with, "Here's what others have found," or, "One challenge some companies deal with is" or, "Let me get your opinion of this."

This is where having a keen understanding of the economic opportunity you provide is extremely helpful. Even companies with seemingly no pain or problems want to save and make money. Whether they have a big budget or no budget, almost every organization will have some funds available if you can demonstrate that your product will help their bottom line.

What may not have been a pain at all might become an urgent desire with proper framing and the right tone. In other words, you can essentially create FOMO (fear of missing out)—whether it be missing out on an opportunity to save money, invest in a more cost effective solution, use a better (more efficient) service, or just acquire a more beautiful/satisfying product altogether.

Most of us have coveted something before, perhaps a beautiful piece of jewelry, an automobile, an article of clothing, or maybe we've regretted not making an investment when given the chance. In reality, FOMO, if strong enough, ultimately becomes a certain kind of pain.

How to Differentiate

A key aspect to your selling success will depend on how well you differentiate yourself from your competition. Using the Opportunity-Solution-Benefits framework will surely help you structure a decent pitch, but to truly excel, you must learn to effectively emphasize the differences between you and your competitors. Drawing a sharp contrast is both necessary and often times difficult.

Knowing your product and market are essential. To draw a contrast, it's imperative to know what's available and how the market looks from the perspective of the buyer. This is table stakes.

Here are three additional ways to help you stand out:

1- Education

In many cases, the buyer may not be as educated or sophisticated as the seller realizes. As a professional seller, you may need to do a better job of educating the buyer on both the product itself, and perhaps even the steps needed to successfully procure the product.

This became evident to me while working on a deal several years ago in Athens, Greece. My point of contact was a highly esteemed professor. Her department was about to be awarded significant funds through a government grant. We had a number of in-depth conversations and Zoom calls over several months. During this process, I came to realize that, although this professor was highly intelligent and educated on matters relating to training and technology, she was rather unfamiliar with the process of buying an expensive piece of equipment and navigating a complicated tender process.

I modified my approach and did my best to educate not only on the technology, but especially on the buying process itself. We developed an excellent rapport and the project was eventually won many months later.

This is just one example specifically relating to the buying process. Regardless of your company or product, you must be able to clearly educate and steer the conversation and dialogue to focus on your strengths. It's imperative to do this in a friendly manner without being condescending.

2- Competition

How you talk about your competitors may be more important than you realize. There's a fair amount of research that's been done on this topic. The overwhelming evidence suggests you should always talk positively about your competition[5].

This can be hard to do, particularly if your competition is legitimately good—or if you've recently lost to them on another deal.

Ignoring (or pretending you don't know) your competition is probably not a winning strategy. Be honest and upfront if the subject arises. In some cases, it might even make sense to bring up your competition if you know that your prospective client has already engaged with them.

The key to talking about your competition is to keep it both positive and brief. Take the high road, and quickly turn the conversation back to your product and company. Here's a simple line that I often use to help reorient the conversation:

"They're a good company. From what I've seen, they do quality work. However, we have a slightly different approach."

This line is an effective set-up that allows you to pivot the conversation and draw an immediate contrast.

3- Stories

It may come as no surprise - stories are an extremely effective way to differentiate yourself from the competition. To be an elite salesperson, you'll need to become an elite storyteller. You'll also need a lot of stories (dozens or more) that you can tell at a moment's notice. Later in the book we'll discuss what I refer to as micro-stories. We'll also go into detail on the types of stories you'll need and where to find them. Stay tuned.

CHAPTER 5

How to
Build Credibility

In this chapter we dive in and focus on some specifics on how to build credibility with buyers who are in the early stage of the Buyer's Journey. Specifically, we focus on those in the awareness phase that need a heavy dose of ethos (credibility).

While the tactics, strategies, and advice in this chapter may be helpful for you as you build out your slide deck and prepare your pitch, the reality is many of the ideas in this chapter will help you build credibility directly and indirectly throughout your entire sales process.

Let's jump into a detailed analogy.

The Reservoir of Credibility

Imagine a beautiful reservoir on a warm summer day. Boaters have come from all around to waterski, wakesurf, swim, and enjoy other recreation. The shores are crowded with bikinis, beach volleyball, and families jockeying for a picnic table under shade trees.

This reservoir is called *Credibility*. When it's completely full, it's irresistible.

However, this reservoir isn't always full—in the early season it's an undesirable place with dirt slopes and muddy swamps.

How do we get the reservoir full? Where does the water that flows into the reservoir originate?

There are two primary tributaries—two rivers—that flow into the reservoir. One is called Company, the other Personal.

Company Credibility

If you're a sales representative of a company with a fantastic reputation, you immediately come into the situation with an advantage.

A quick online search reveals that some of the most reputable companies over the last few decades include Apple, Google, Microsoft, and Disney. Imagine you're in a B2B environment, trying to sell something as a representative from one of those companies—you have a certain amount of instant credibility bestowed upon you. In this case, the reservoir has already been (mostly) filled. Just don't screw it up!

I was once at a conference in Anaheim, California, at the Disneyland Hotel. The conference itself was rather boring, but the closing keynote speaker was a senior vice president from the Disneyland Resort. The company he represented, and his title immediately gave him some credibility. People put down their phones and listened to his talk, which (as I recall) was an interesting list of "Things You Might Not Know about Disneyland." To his credit, his speech was engaging, although ultimately, it was just a veiled pitch about why you should vacation at the Magic Kingdom.

It obviously worked—several months later, I took my kids to Disneyland.

Although most of us don't work for Disney, Apple, Google, or Microsoft, if you are representing a company, hopefully that company's reputation provides you with a net positive reputation within your specific industry.

The truth is there are a lot of factors that impact a company's reputation. Marketing and advertising, branding strategy, and word of mouth are huge factors. Company history and time/tenure in the market are considerations as well. A company's presence at industry conferences and trade shows also makes a difference. Even the earned reputation (good or bad) of company executives and current (and former) employees can impact the reputation and credibility of a company.

As sellers, we need to be aware of the reputation of our company, but also cognizant that we may not be able to impact the flow from this "river" into the reservoir of credibility.

Personal Credibility

Whereas an individual salesperson may not have control over the reputation of the company they represent, they have full control over their personal credibility. Even in a situation where there's little or no credibility flowing from a company, it's possible for a salesperson to gain enough credibility in the eyes of the buyer to fill the reservoir completely.

There's a lot that goes into personal credibility. As we evaluate the flow of this river, we quickly realize there are many branches and tributaries to this river. What are they?

In 2023, while researching and writing this book, I decided to conduct a survey to further understand the factors that contribute to personal credibility.

Hundreds of participants were asked the following question:

Assume you are making a large and important purchase on behalf of your company or organization. During the process, you must carefully evaluate a number of different vendors. You must also work closely with a sales professional from each vendor.

In your opinion, what are the ideal traits and characteristics of a sales professional?

Rate each characteristic on a scale between 1 and 10 (with 10 being the highest rating)

Competence

Not surprisingly, competence was the top answer. Buyers want to work with somebody who is competent and possesses the knowledge to assist them and answer their questions. They can detect when a salesperson is failing to understand their situation and needs.

According to Challenger research, buyers expect an "Insight-led sales experience. They are hungry for value, unique insights about their business, and for sales professionals capable of serving as true business partners."

The sales experience (and the competence of the sales professional) is the number one driver that leads to customer loyalty. Buyers consider the sales experience a more important factor when making a purchase than a company's reputation, the price, or even the product itself.[6]

How to Increase Competence

One of the best ways for a salesperson to exhibit competence is to ask insightful questions of the prospective customer and then be able to engage in a conversational dialogue.

To give a very broad example, a salesperson may ask a question such as the following:

"Help me understand, Mr. Customer. At your company, when it comes to X, do you prefer THIS approach or THAT approach?"

Customer then responds with an answer.

Salesperson then responds. "Very interesting. What I've seen throughout the industry is that THIS approach usually works well for many organizations because of (reason 1 and reason 2), but it sounds like your situation is a little bit different. Why?"

When a salesperson engages in such a dialogue, it exhibits a level of competence. The goal is to get the prospective customer to feel like they've gained some insight from the salesperson—who they (hopefully) begin to view as more of a trusted advisor or consultant—and less of someone with "sales" or "business development" in their title.

Reliability

Reliability was the #2 rated characteristic in the survey. Reliability largely comes down to responsiveness to the needs of the prospective customer. Are phone calls answered? Are messages returned in a timely manner? Are meetings scheduled and attended on time?

In B2B sales, the process can be months or even years long. However, there are often phases and moments during the process where the buyer needs attention.

Many times, after a proposal is sent, it may sit on a decision-maker's desk for weeks without any consideration. Follow-up calls may go unanswered. Then, seemingly out of nowhere, a salesperson receives a call and a request to answer some highly technical questions.

The problem for the salesperson is that they may be traveling or attending a conference during the week of this request. A reliable response may require some inconvenient internal calls and some late nights crafting a detailed message in a hotel room.

At the very least, it requires reliable correspondence and communication with the prospective customer to manage expectations.

How to Increase Reliability

Reliability matters even when it's inconvenient. In most sales roles it requires a certain amount of discipline. Following up with a customer and staying committed to a process is key. Keeping the CRM and personal task list up to date is a big part of the equation.

I have often told colleagues and employees that, as a sales manager, I would rather have a sales professional on my team who is an all-star at following up but has only average presentation skills than a sales professional who is an all-star presenter and is only average at following up.

Likability

The number three trait is likability. There's an old saying that's popular in the world of sales—"People do business with those they know, like, and trust."

However, there has been some debate in recent years among sales gurus and experts in the realm of B2B sales on whether likability really matters anymore.

This may stem from some content in the popular book *The Challenger Sale*. In the book, the authors make a compelling case that B2B sales professionals can be categorized into one of five different groups:

- Relationship Builder
- Reactive Problem Solver
- Hard Worker
- Lone Wolf
- Challenger

Not surprisingly, the book makes the argument that the Challenger sales professional is the most effective. This type of salesperson takes control of a sale and teaches their prospects how to solve their problems rather than spending a long time building relationships.

The Challenger salesperson is all about competence—a trait that we've already identified as the #1 most important trait to build credibility.

The problem with the book *The Challenger Sale* is not the content or approach. It's the interpretation. Many read the book and seem to walk away thinking that relationships and likability are not important.

My own research and experience would strongly suggest that's the wrong interpretation.

Yes, the Challenger approach is valid. Competence matters. I'm personally an advocate of teaching, tailoring, and taking control (as taught in *The Challenger Sale*).

I also believe that relationships and likability are still important aspects of selling. You don't have to be an arrogant jerk to adhere to the Challenger approach.

The old adage, "People buy from those they know, like, and trust," is not mutually exclusive from the Challenger methodology. The two can co-exist together.

There is an interesting facet of likability. In my survey, while likability was the third most popular trait that enhanced a salesperson's overall credibility, in the United States of America, likability was ranked #2, just after competence but before reliability. The evidence certainly suggests that Americans in particular seem to prefer likable sales professionals.

Sales guru and popular podcast host Andy Paul perhaps said it best during a discussion about likability on *The Win Rate Podcast* stating that "likability costs you nothing" as a salesperson. I fully agree. There are some who might spend considerable time, energy, and money on learning the latest and greatest sales strategies and proper questions to ask during a complex B2B sales process—yet they dismiss the easy advantage they could gain by just being a bit more pleasant and likable. In an era where product and technology differences are often hard to distinguish, likability could be more important than ever.

How to Increase Likability

There are a variety of ways to increase one's likability. Inasmuch as it's an important aspect of credibility and perhaps a little more nuanced than competence and reliability, it's worthwhile to explore likability in greater depth.

Conversational Ability

Can you easily converse with a prospective customer—not just when engaged in a presentation, but during the before and after? The banter and chitchat that occur at the beginning and end of a meeting are opportunities to establish rapport. Lunch and dinner meetings represent more opportunities to communicate and correspond with a prospective client.

The ability to listen during a conversation and ask meaningful questions based on a person's response is essential. If there's an awkward silence, can you jump-start the conversation or make an observation that will get a person talking? This is not a particularly difficult skill to learn, but it requires some practice to come off naturally.

I've personally found there are three topics almost anyone, anywhere in the world will happily discuss (sometimes at length). These topics are easy to bring up almost anytime and can spur additional conversation that helps build rapport:

1. Hometown. Almost everyone will be willing to talk about their hometown if you show genuine curiosity and ask thoughtful questions. Start by asking, "Where are you from?" Follow up by asking any number of related questions: "What is your hometown best known for?" "How big is your hometown?" "What is the primary industry your hometown is best known for?"

2. Food. Everyone eats, and almost everyone has an opinion about food. Just try asking someone for a lunch or dinner recommendation. Regardless of where you are in the world, people will have an opinion of where to go and what to eat. It's almost always a conversation starter and is often paired with questions about somebody's hometown. If you want to endear yourself to someone, providing a sincere compliment about someone's hometown or about the local cuisine can go a long way.

3. Travel. This is another topic that most folks love to discuss. People love to talk about their vacations and where they travel—or where they wish to travel. It's really easy to pivot from a boring weather conversation to a more interesting travel conversation. If someone says, "Weather's really bad outside today," it's easy to remark, "Yes, it is. I wish I was at the beach. Where do you usually go to get away from the bad weather?"

There is a fourth topic you can use to spur a conversation, but it's riskier. Nevertheless, it's a topic that can, if you've done your research, really open up a dialogue. The topic is competition. More specifically, what company is the competition. If you're on the phone or in a business meeting, just try asking about the competition. If you've done your research, you can even mention the competitor's name. You may capture some immediate attention or evoke a reaction. This can be a great transition topic that can build rapport and open a meaningful dialogue. I've used this very effectively at times. For most companies, this is a serious topic, and ears will usually perk up when you start to talk about their competitors. When I do this, it's usually with a curious tone—but it often works with great impact.

In one instance, I was presenting to a group of executives and managers in a large board room. My CEO happened to be accompanying me in the meeting. We spent the first ten minutes engaged in introductions and small talk—but the conversation started getting a bit stale. I pivoted by mentioning that we both had a common competitor, and then I mentioned the competitor's name and some facts about the company. Everyone in the room was immediately attentive—there was an instant rapport that developed as everyone realized we were engaged in the same battle against a common competitor.

Later that day, my CEO went out of his way to tell me, "That was the perfect thing to say at the perfect time."

Body Language: The Sunrise-Sunset Theory

Body language and positioning are two more aspects of likability that are subtly important when trying to build rapport and avoid awkwardness in a sales setting.

Many people think of body language in the context of public speaking—those best practices are fairly well known: stand tall, maintain good posture, make eye contact with your audience, avoid hands in your pockets.

The context that is just as important and perhaps lesser known is body language and positioning in a smaller, more intimate setting. Think of a one-on-one interview or sales presentation to a small group around a conference table. How are you positioned? What are you doing with your hands and arms?

I teach a concept called the *sunrise-sunset theory of body language.* The concept is simple. Think of the sun at high noon—it's right above you—the heat and light are harsh and uncomfortable. By contrast, the light at sunrise (or sunset) is much more pleasant, beautiful, warm, and not overbearing.

In an intimate business setting, such as a sales presentation or interview, you never want to position yourself right in front of someone. Like the sun at noon—it's too direct and too harsh. The last thing you want to do is come across as overbearing. Even if your tone and content are on target, there's often a subconscious resistance or awkwardness that can occur when you're nose to nose with somebody—even if you're a few feet away (such as across the table). Try adjusting your position so you're never directly in front of somebody in an overbearing posture.

I've seen door-to-door sales professionals who have mastered this art. Think of a typical door approach—it begins with an assertive nose-to-nose position. Skilled door-to-door professionals are keenly aware this is one of the many challenges they face trying to build rapport in seconds as they deliver their pitch. Many times, they will introduce themselves and then, just a few seconds later, turn their body ninety degrees while pointing down the street and referencing somebody in the neighborhood who purchased their product. I've also seen them pull out a brochure and use it as a visual aid while they position themselves (almost) side by side with the homeowner. This is a method designed to cut the subtle tension that is naturally present when we're face-to-face with someone—particularly a stranger.

This body language theory is not going to automatically win you any deal. What we're going for is likability—and this is a small tip, one of perhaps dozens to be aware of as you're making an impression and trying to build likability and rapport with a prospective client.

Body Language as a Listener

Another aspect of body language that's not often taught is the type of body language you should be exhibiting when another person is talking. This is particularly important in an intimate sales conversation, when you're presenting to a small group, asking questions, and listening to responses.

Your ability to nod and smile at the right moment can be critical in helping to encourage a response. It also shows engagement and curiosity. Most of the time a head nod is a semi-conscious action—we may not realize its importance. Research shows that "head nodding plays an important role in regulating an interaction, signaling who is to take a turn or whether or not someone is interested in and attending to a particular item."[7]

A subtle left-right nod can also send a message to put the brakes on an interaction.

I had a somewhat embarrassing realization of the importance of nodding many years ago during a business meeting in Ahmedabad, India.

Throughout India there's a gesture known as the head wobble (or head shake) that's frequently used as an acknowledgment during a face-to-face conversation. In Western cultures, a verbal acknowledgment (such as "yeah") along with a slight up-and-down head nod is common during a conversation and is a signal from the recipient to the speaker that you understand and for them to continue speaking. But in India, a slight head bobble—that often presents like a diagonal head nod—serves the same purpose.

During my business meeting I was presenting to an executive who spoke excellent English but kept giving me this unfamiliar head nod. I thought he misheard me or didn't understand the concept—so I repeated it back to him. This continued several more times during the course of the meeting—and I was getting somewhat frustrated. Then another executive walked into the room, and I observed them both giving the same head nod gesture to each other in a casual way. I soon caught on and stopped repeating myself—having learned a valuable lesson on the finer details of non-verbal communication in India.

The real takeaway for me was gaining a better understanding of the importance of non-verbal cues, specifically head nods and facial expressions, during a sales interaction. When they're not present, or when the wrong expressions and head nods are sent, it can create confusion or send negative signals. You may be an excellent presenter and ask terrific questions, but if you don't act engaged and interested during your prospective buyer's response, your likability will take a hit.

Winning Friends

Beyond being conversational and having good body language and positioning, there are so many other aspects to likability: humor, personality, generosity.

There are many books written on the subject, and perhaps most notable is Dale Carnegie's legendary *How to Win Friends and Influence People*, which is probably even more relevant today than it was when it was first released in 1936. While the entire book is worth a read every few years (as a refresher for virtually anyone in the business world), it's worth noting the six key principles as outlined in part 2 of the book: "Six Ways to Make People Like You."

1- Become Genuinely Interested in other people

2- Smile

3- Remember that a person's name is (to that person) the sweetest and most important sound in any language.

4- Be a good listener. Encourage others to talk about themselves.

5- Talk in terms of the other person's interests.

6- Make the other person feel important—and do it sincerely.

Authenticity

While authenticity is ranked fourth in the survey, in many ways it may be the most important. Why? In many sales situations it takes at least some time for a prospective buyer to get a true gauge on the competence, reliability, and likability of a salesperson, whereas authenticity (or lack thereof) can usually be detected quickly.

Going back for a moment to our reservoir analogy. Authenticity is a nice little stream that flows into our reservoir of credibility, but there's something different about authenticity. If it's off, even just slightly, it can be quickly and easily detected. This stream can literally turn salty and smell like sulfur. It can spoil the entire reservoir!

On Christmas Eve of 1994, I was a college student working at my first real sales job. For several months, I had been working evenings and weekends at Fleet Foot, an athletic shoe store in a suburban mall near Salt Lake City. This shoe store was very much like a Foot Locker on steroids, with hundreds of athletic shoes spanning the walls. Thousands more were stacked in the back room ready to be sold. This was at the height of the '90s when Air Jordans, Air Barkleys, and Shaq's Reebok high-tops were all the rage.

As a commissioned sales representative, I had a base wage of $7 per hour, and (on most days) I also made a 2 percent commission on gross sales. However, on especially busy days, it was possible to sell over $2,000 of product, and if a salesperson broke through the $2,000 mark, they received a bump to 4 percent commission on gross sales.

Christmas Eve was certainly going to be an opportunity to break the $2,000 barrier. Keep in mind, this was before Amazon and Zappos. Most people hadn't heard of the internet in 1994, much less purchased anything online. If you wanted to buy shoes for a Christmas gift, you pretty much needed to go to a shopping mall.

I drove to work excited that morning. But there were some challenges—on Christmas Eve, the mall closed three hours early. Also, our store was going to be fully staffed. Adam, Hank, Danny, Shane, Rob, and Bianca were all going to be working on Christmas Eve, trying to manage the rush. Breaking the $2,000 barrier would take some serious hustle!

At 8:30 a.m., we had a quick sales meeting. Then, just as we were wrapping up, about five minutes before the store was set to open, a lady in her mid-sixties approached the front gate. She gently tapped a few times and then briskly asked, "Can I get some help? I need some shoes." I happened to be in the right place, situated near the front of the store, and I quickly walked over to assist her as my manager opened the gate.

What a stroke of luck! Ninety-five percent of the time, when an elderly lady comes into an athletic shoe store, it's to purchase some Air Jordans for her grandson. This was a "bluebird deal" or (as we called it back then) a "birthday sale" because every so often a grandmother would come in and purchase a pair of athletic shoes for her grandson as a birthday gift. Usually it was a quick sale—no trying on shoes, no special requests, just ringing up the old lady for a pair of Air Jordans. Of course, on this day, the occasion wasn't a birthday. It was Christmas—and I was going to get a quick head start on the rest of the team. As I said, stroke of luck!

Except, to my surprise, this lady didn't ask for Air Jordans for her grandson. She was interested in trying on some New Balance walking shoes. After a few minutes she asked to try on some Reebok Club C sneakers (some of the least expensive shoes in the store). I went back and forth from the stockroom at least three times trying to find the right size and style for this lady. By now the store had opened, and Bianca and Adam, my two top rivals, had already rung up a customer. I was getting anxious and frustrated. The lady walked back and forth to the mirror, then approached me again, asking for yet another style.

I'm not sure exactly what I did at that point. Perhaps I mumbled something under my breath or gave a teenage eye roll before going back to grab the sneakers. When I returned, the old lady was talking with my manager. She didn't mince any words, "I want another salesperson," she loudly demanded. "I want someone who doesn't only care about their commission."

My manager, eager to calm the situation and avoid any escalation, motioned me away and introduced Bianca, one of my co-workers. Bianca finished helping the lady as she slipped on the shoes I had brought out moments earlier. After a brief discussion with my manager in the back room, where I explained my side of the story, I walked back out to help another customer.

A few minutes later, out of the corner of my eye, I noticed Bianca was ringing up the old lady at the cash register. To my surprise, the lady walked out of the store with (what looked like) two shoe boxes in her bag. Once she exited, I walked over to the register where Bianca proudly explained she had not only sold the lady the white sneakers but also some Air Jordans for her grandson. The total transaction value was over $150. Worse—I had just allowed a rival to jump ahead of me.

The real insult to injury occurred several hours later. As the store closed, we calculated the final daily sales totals. My total was $1,900, and Bianca had just barely broken $2,000. She got the big Christmas commission. I went home a little dejected—all because of the incident that morning. My antics—however slight—were like salt water and sulfur to that lady. She had detected my inauthenticity, my salesy-ness, and it was a massive turnoff to her, as it is to almost any prospective customer.

The Original Sin of Selling

Whether in retail, B2B, or anywhere in between, most professional salespeople know and understand the virtues of being authentic and not projecting commission breath. Yet, I'm still surprised at how often I see tactics and techniques being used that amplify salesy-ness. This seems especially true in industries where the buying cycle is short and sales are more transactional in nature.

Assumptive sales tactics, one-time offers, bait-and-switch techniques, false scarcity, and other emotionally manipulative sales tactics are far from extinct.

As we briefly discussed in Chapter 3, being "salesy" is the original sin of selling. The less we act like a salesperson, the more authentic and sincere we are in our interactions, the more likely we are to have success.

Should You Withhold the Price?

One commonly used tactic that is taught far and wide is withholding pricing when somebody asks. There are many schools of thought regarding this strategy. One side argues that salespeople should always freely give out a price, as, typically, this type of information is widely available online. Providing transparent pricing can help build credibility and seems ethical. The other side argues that giving out pricing too early gives the consumer too much power to shop for the best deal and creates a race to the bottom. It can also create problems, particularly with more complex sales, where proper research and discovery are necessary to provide an accurate quotation.

If you're a sales professional, how do you handle a pricing question? The answer is, it depends. It depends upon your industry and your strategy. This is often a topic that requires some proper training. However, there are *wrong* ways to handle this type of question. The wrong way is to withhold pricing in a way that causes salesy-ness. Yet, it happens all the time, when a poorly trained salesperson is asked, "What's the price?" And they withhold their answer in an insincere, questionable manner.

Withholding the price, particularly when a potential customer is in the research phase of the Buyer's Journey and is thirsting for information, can create awkwardness and mistrust and comes across as salesy. Sales professionals must be trained on how to manage this question. Typically, the approach is to answer in the affirmative, then follow up with some discovery questions such as follows:

- "Are you looking for the complete solution, or for a limited version?"

- "Do you need customizations?"

- "How many are you looking for?"

- "What options do you want?"

- "How soon do you need it?"

These are just a few basic questions, and ideally, you can be more specific and drill down. Most of the time, a prospective buyer will engage with you—but they typically expect some sort of answer. When they persist in knowing the price, you, as the sales professional, now have more information and are in a better position to answer their question. Many times, the response involves a price range rather than a specific number. When pressed hard, this is typically an easy way to answer the price question in a not-so-salesy way. Provide a general range, and then follow up with discovery questions. The real key is to never act salesy—don't tap into the salt water that smells of sulfur. As a general rule, it's far better to give away a little too much pricing information a little too soon rather than come across as a smarmy salesperson.

The Tension "Takeaway" Tactic

Regardless of the industry, there will often come instances where you're not trusted as a salesperson. It's natural for people to feel uncomfortable around salespeople. This is true even in the most high-brow industries, even when a salesperson is providing insight and education in a consultative manner. Sometimes people have an aura of skepticism and hesitancy when they're interacting with you. It may be inherent, or it may be something you've said or done that raises caution in their demeanor. Oftentimes, you can literally detect the tension in the air. The person you're pitching, your captive audience, has detected a certain "salesy-ness" and they don't like it.

What can you do? Is there a strategy or a tactic you can use to dial down tension? An aerosol you can spray to reduce the stench of salesy-ness?

The answer is yes. I learned this strategy early in my career and have used it more times than I can remember. It's not foolproof, but most of the time it works brilliantly. It's called the *tension takeaway.*

Let me give a proper background to this strategy.

First—think of the most salesy profession in the world. Door-to-door? Insurance? Car sales? If you ask me, a strong candidate for such an award would be a timeshare salesperson.

Believe it or not, I was a licensed timeshare sales professional for a brief period in the late 1990s. This was just a few years after my stint in the retail shoe business. At the time, I was living in Las Vegas, Nevada. Still in college, I was navigating a full schedule and needed a job where I could work nights while attending classes in the morning. A resort located about a mile west of the Las Vegas Strip advertised a high-paying sales job in the local classifieds. I showed up to apply and was pretty much offered the job on the spot. It was 100 percent commission, and I needed to pass a real estate exam, but the hours worked perfectly with my schedule.

Here's a brief synopsis of the timeshare business, for those who are unfamiliar. A real estate company (usually in a touristy destination such as Las Vegas) decides to sell ownership in a condominium resort. Rather than sell a condominium outright, the resort sells individual weeks during the year to tourists and vacationers. If you own a timeshare, you visit the destination each year during your allotted week. Modern timeshares are typically affiliated with a global network that allows the owner to trade their week and visit other resorts in different destinations throughout the world. Of course, there are a lot of fees involved—typically, most financial experts (and the general public) believe that ownership in a timeshare is NOT a great investment, unless you always travel to the same destination year after year.

The business itself is pure sales—often of the high-pressure variety. Here's the setup: A "marketing representative" from the timeshare company approaches a couple in a high-traffic area on the Las Vegas strip.

They offer a free gift (usually tickets to an evening show) if the couple is willing to listen to a ninety-minute sales presentation. If the couple agrees, they're whisked away minutes later in a shuttle van to the resort.

Upon arriving at the resort, the couple heads into a luxurious waiting room where they're soon introduced to a sales associate. Once they've greeted their sales associate, they're ushered into a bright and airy sales lounge where dozens of other couples are situated at small circular tables. The atmosphere in the room is festive, music is playing, and free soda and hot cookies are being served.

Typically, a sales associate sits down with the couple and spends the first ten minutes chitchatting about travel and their likes and dislikes. Over the next sixty to ninety minutes, they watch a promotional video and tour the resort area, and then the sales pitch goes full throttle. Near the end of the presentation, a sales manager (closer) comes in and often dials up the pressure with hopes of securing a deal.

My experience working at the timeshare resort was relatively short. It was a job of convenience that lasted less than a year. However, I had a reasonable amount of success for a young sales associate. I was by no means the top salesperson of the forty to fifty sales professionals employed at the resort. But for my age (at the time I was in my early twenties), I did reasonably well—especially considering I was only working part-time and was nearly two decades younger than the average salesperson.

Part of my success in that job I attribute to my trainer, a middle-aged guy named Chuck who took me under his wing during the first three weeks of training. Chuck told me about a concept called *the takeaway*, which he referred to as a reverse psychology tactic.

Anyone familiar with old-school sales tactics has probably heard of the takeaway, also known as the *takeaway close* or *takeaway selling*. There's a wide variety of applications on how to use this approach—some of them are cringeworthy.

These old tactics are *not* what I was taught when selling timeshares. The tension takeaway I learned (and still use) is more proactive. Rather than taking something away (as is typically done with a takeaway approach) I was instructed to simply take away the sales pressure. But how?

Let's go back to the timeshare sales lounge. Every couple that comes through the door knows they're being pitched. They're expecting a high-pressure sales presentation given by a slick salesperson. As a salesperson, acknowledging the situation in front of the buyers and immediately telling them, "You don't have to buy today," dials down that tension almost immediately.

I got really good at using the tension takeaway. To supercharge this approach, you must do it as nonchalantly as possible. I learned to give off not even a whiff of sales desperation as I explained to people, "You don't have to buy today." Once I did this, my commission breath disappeared, and the door opened, just slightly, for me to build up credibility throughout the rest of the presentation.

Skillfully using this approach helped me punch above my weight during my time as a timeshare sales associate. One day, when it was a little bit slow, one of my coworkers, Tony, approached me in the break room. He was one of the company's top sellers, and he was complimentary and congratulated me on a big deal I had closed a day earlier. Tony sat down in front of me and wanted to talk about the sales strategy and technique I used to "box in" the customer. He was surprised when I told him I didn't use a "box-them-in" strategy—I sold it straight up.

During my entire time selling timeshare, I never needed to use high-pressure tactics. I focused on building rapport, taking away any sales tension, showing enthusiasm, and then accurately showcasing the merits and advantages of the program. That was enough to be relatively successful as a part-time timeshare sales professional.

The truth is, timeshare was never going to be a career for me, but had I stayed and focused my efforts full-time, I'm convinced I would have eventually been a top dog at the resort, without "boxing in" any prospective customers.

Perhaps it's a bad pun, but the real "takeaway" from my stint selling timeshare was the tension takeaway tactic. It was a simple strategy that helped cut the friction and reduce the salesy-ness of a situation. I took what I learned and applied it a few months later in my next role selling web and marketing services. Although it was a very different industry, the takeaway tactic worked.

I've found that takeaway tactic works in virtually every industry and in every culture—and I've now been using it for twenty-five years. I was recently in northern Italy, meeting with some executives from a large training organization interested in buying a training simulator. Early in our meeting, I could detect through the thick Italian accent and the tension in the room that two of the executives had some trepidation. I paused for a moment and immediately explained to them, word for word, the following:

"Just so you are aware, you don't need to buy anything from me today. Even if you want it, nobody ever writes a check on the first day. I will just explain and show you the product, and you can decide if you want it or not."

This statement transformed me, in their eyes, from a sketchy foreign salesperson to a friendly consultant educating them on simulators. Sixty minutes later, we were laughing together while eating pasta at the local trattoria. Two weeks later, they placed an order.

Using the Right Tone

Before we move on from authenticity, we need to address tonality when communicating in a sales situation.

It's very possible to say all the right words during a presentation or call and still come across as insincere.

All too often sales professionals, especially early in their careers, focus on memorizing a script and saying the right words, without paying much attention to the pace and overall tone of their voice.

Veteran sales professionals are not immune to these mistakes. I completely missed the mark just last year during a stop-in visit with an important contact. Yes, even though I have a plethora of experience meeting, greeting, and presenting to people around the world, and despite the fact that I practice my skills frequently and train others on this topic, I still screwed up and ruined a good opportunity by using the wrong tone.

This mishap occurred in Jacksonville, Florida. My prospect (let's call him Larry) had been virtually impossible for me to get in touch with for years. Larry was the executive director for a large, well-funded organization. I am personally acquainted and (in many cases) good friends with almost every other executive director in this niche industry. Larry was the only hold-out. He was never willing to engage in a conversation and skipped most industry conferences.

One afternoon, when passing through Jacksonville, I stopped by his office unannounced. Moments later, to my surprise, he came out to the reception area to greet me. Honestly, I was a bit startled to see him—he had been so evasive for years. I open my mouth . . .

"Hey, how ya doin'?"

I almost sounded like Joey from the sitcom *Friends*.

My tone was too excited; my pace was too fast. I had also been caught off guard and was somewhat unprepared.

I quickly gathered my thoughts and told him something educational and interesting relating to our industry. I then followed up with a question, asking specifically about a person I knew was a mutual acquaintance.

My question was perfect, and the dialogue was good enough, but my tone and cadence were a mile off.

I could immediately tell by his body language and the look on his face that I had missed the mark. There was tension in the air, a wall of resistance.

I'd come in way too excited, too salesy, especially for an unannounced visit to his office.

Larry hastily answered my inquiry about the mutual acquaintance and then mumbled something about it not being a good time to meet.

I tried asking another question, but he was already trying to disengage—glancing over his shoulder and then down at his watch.

The whole interaction lasted about ninety seconds. He accepted my business card and brochure, but the visit was an utter failure.

Walking back to my car, I was in a bit of shock. But it only took me a minute or two to replay the situation in my mind and realize my fatal flaw: it was all in the tone of my voice and the pace of my words.

If I could repeat the exact scenario again—walking in to greet Larry—I'm absolutely convinced I could engage him in a meaningful conversation. Here's the thing: I probably wouldn't even have to change any of the words, just the tone and pace of my voice. Rather than an excited, fast-paced tone, I should have used a slow, curious, and inquisitive tone. I'm 100 percent sure the interaction would have had a better outcome.

Acting Too Excited and Talking Too Fast

Excitement may seem like a positive attribute, but in many sales situations, particularly when we're talking about the tone and inclination of your voice, it's better to sound more neutral. An excited and energetic tone of voice is too salesy. This is especially true when greeting someone for the first time or starting your presentation.

If you're speaking to an audience, there's a natural tendency to talk fast. Instead, try speaking slowly and deliberately. Don't be afraid to pause.

This is not new advice. Well-known author and FBI negotiator Chris Voss recommends using a "slow, late-night FM DJ voice" during negotiations. I believe this is brilliant advice, but I would add, it's not only during negotiations—but most sales interactions. You should be using a slower pace with a curious, inquisitive, and accommodating tone.

I've packaged together a lot under the banner of authenticity in this section, but I believe it's critically important to building relationships and selling. Much like the starter in your car, it may not be the most important part of the vehicle—that would be the engine, transmission, and wheels—but without the starter, you're not going anywhere.

In professional sales, as our survey has shown, credibility, reliability, and likability may ultimately be more important. But authenticity is the starter—without it, you may never have the opportunity to show your credibility, reliability, and likability. It doesn't matter if you're selling simulators in Italy, timeshares in Las Vegas, or Air Jordans in a suburban mall, seek to be authentic, and avoid salesy-ness at all costs.

Confidence

The fifth most important attribute is confidence. There's an interesting aspect to confidence when it comes to credibility. You must have the right amount. Too much confidence can be perceived as arrogance, which will hurt your likability. Too little confidence and the prospective buyer may view you as incompetent—which is potentially even more problematic.

In our reservoir analogy, confidence is yet another tributary—and this is one where it's important to watch the water level. Have you ever been to a lake or reservoir that's recently flooded? It's usually not a desirable place.

You'll find debris, branches, logs, and oftentimes trash in the water.

The key is to build confidence in yourself without being showy or cocky in front of prospective customers or your peers.

You Must Eat Your Own Dog Food

One key to showing confidence is believing and doing what you say. I had a boss who continually referred to this as "eating your own dog food." Funny notion, but he was right: You must believe in what you sell. Ideally, you're not just a salesperson, but a consumer of whatever it is that you offer. At the very least, you must believe whatever you are selling will provide some benefit to the recipient. If you're lying or faking it, you may fool people temporarily—perhaps you'll even close the sale—but it's a bad recipe. People can often detect when you're faking confidence—particularly when the stakes are high.

What if you're offering or selling something that isn't the best product or solution that's available? That's OK. There are Mercedes Benzes in the world and there are Chevrolets. If you happen to be selling a Chevrolet, you don't have to believe it's a better car than a Mercedes—but you do have to believe it provides a certain value and utility for some buyers. The truth is, for many people, a Chevrolet is a better car.

Though we just spoke about tone in the previous section, tone and language can impact how confident you are in the eyes of the prospective buyer. The inflection of your sentences can make a real difference.

Avoid Uptalk

Uptalk is a common problem among sales professionals where an upward inflection at the end of a sentence is used to imply a question.

Uptalk can be used effectively, particularly as a mirroring technique. But some people tend to use uptalk without knowing, which can give the impression they lack confidence and knowledge.

I've also seen instances where uptalk can come across as slightly condescending. One executive I knew occasionally used an upward inflecting "Okay?" at the end of a statement. He would be giving instructions or an explanation, and then before moving on to the next topic, this awkward "Okay?" would slip out like he was looking for an affirmative response from a group of kindergartners.

These issues of tone, confidence, and authenticity can be practiced and easily improved upon. Too often, sales professionals only practice when they're live with a prospective client. We're always firing live bullets, never training or practicing our craft. The giving and receiving of feedback is something that is lacking in almost every sales organization. Those companies that bake in training, pitch practice, role-playing, and proactive feedback will not only see greater success in the long run but also will gain more confidence collectively as a group and as individual sales professionals.

Credibility Is a Marathon

While there could be an entire book written on the importance of credibility in the context of sales and customer success, there is one last key point and one final story that must be written here to wrap up our reservoir analogy and conclude this chapter.

Credibility is a marathon, not a sprint. It's usually built over a considerable amount of time. Just as a reservoir rarely fills quickly—it happens over the course of weeks or months—credibility in the B2B world and even the B2C world should be looked at through a farsighted lens.

Oftentimes, marketing professionals seem to understand this more intuitively than sales professionals, who are often motivated and influenced by commissions and sales funnels. Marketers know and understand the importance of dripping on a lead or prospect, knowing that multiple points of exposure increases the chances for success, whereas sales professionals are often antsy and impatient creatures—striking when the iron is hot, but sometimes quick to drop a contact from the active sales funnel if they're not progressing fast enough.

Sometimes it's forgotten that in many industries, the biggest competitor is "no decision" and a prospective client may have just postponed or otherwise delayed a purchase for a period of time.

Pipelines and prospects may come and go, but exposure and credibility are slowly gained month after month and year after year. This is why I'm not a fan of break-up emails or burning any bridges with prospects that may have bought from a competitor.

Mining Old Leads

One strategy I advocate is mining old leads. This has worked for me in multiple industries and at multiple companies. Specifically, I like to find leads that were once promising prospects but (for whatever reason) fell out of the sales funnel and were ultimately forgotten. Almost every company has orphan customers, contacts, or leads. You may have to go deep into the CRM system to find them, but it's amazing how much old gold is buried in your own backyard! In many cases, the reservoir of credibility is already partially filled with these old legacy contacts. Selling becomes a bit easier when you already have a head start!

The Power of a Sincere Mea Culpa

Of course, there are instances where you run into a disenfranchised former customer. This was the case once when I reached out to an old contact in a company database and called up Barbara—an extremely sharp, no-nonsense

New Yorker who basically hung up the phone on me after thirty seconds.

I was baffled by the call.

Records showed that her organization had spent over a million dollars purchasing two flagship systems from our company just a decade earlier. Now, for whatever reason, the relationship was ice cold. I was also surprised at how little knowledge any of my colleagues had about this former client. It was a bit of a company mystery. Nobody really knew what had gone wrong.

A couple of months later I was in New York, and I reached out to Barbara to see if I could swing by her office for a face-to-face meeting. She was slightly more cordial—but declined.

I made it a habit to call Barbara once every quarter. Sometimes I just left a message to tell her I was in the New York area. Occasionally we spoke—usually just for a minute—and our conversations were short but becoming more friendly.

Finally, about eighteen months after my initial inquiry, she called me out of the blue to ask me when I was going to be in New York again. I met with her a couple of weeks later in person. We had an enlightening conversation where I learned a few details that helped solve the mystery.

Her organization had indeed spent over a million dollars on two state-of-the-art simulators a decade earlier. Several years went by and she was a happy client, but a minor problem turned into a heated dispute over a warranty claim. The situation turned sour when a former executive at my company reneged on some agreements. There was apparently some gray area in the negotiations, but my company had acted in bad faith (according to Barbara). Turns out, the executive involved left our company a few years later (for unrelated reasons) and never communicated his side of the story. But none of that mattered to Barbara, or anyone in her organizat ion. In their eyes, my company had little to no credibility.

Barbara then informed me that they were once again evaluating different simulators and technology solutions for training. She also explicitly told me that, because of our history, they were strongly favoring our competitor. It would be a long shot for me to win the deal.

Armed with this new information, I went back and informed my team and went to work on a proposal and plan. Five weeks later I showed up with my new CEO to deliver a demonstration over a three-day period. Our technology showed well with the rank-and-file employees, but many of Barbara's management team (particularly the old-timers who knew of the previous situation) were a bit skittish.

On the last day, I gave a presentation to a group of senior managers and decision-makers in an auditorium. After a thirty-second introduction, I cleared the air:

"I know several years ago there was a dispute regarding a warranty with one of our former executives. I'm not exactly sure what went wrong, but on behalf of my company, I apologize, and I promise to make it right. If you select our company for this project, we'll double the initial warranty from twelve months to twenty-four months, no questions asked."

I looked around the room—every single person was writing down what I had just told them. Half of them were nodding their heads affirmatively.

Opening my presentation with a mea culpa was the right move. To this day, I consider that presentation one of the best I have given in my entire career. I had spent months slowly building up credibility with Barbara, and I had earned the opportunity to present to her team. With the mea culpa, I was now in good standing with the other important decision-makers.

It took several more months to win the deal, but ultimately, Barbara placed an order for over US$1.5 million. Since that time, she has been an extremely loyal customer who has provided me with many positive referrals and references.

I tell this story to illustrate that credibility and trust are earned—but often (particularly in B2B sales), it takes months or years to fill that reservoir.

Proactively Putting Yourself in the Spotlight

There is one additional way to enhance your personal credibility, and it can be an enormous game changer for those who are willing to make the effort.

Become an expert.

Today it's easier than ever to put yourself in the spotlight and ultimately become recognized as an expert within your field. This can take courage, but you can build an enormous amount of credibility with complete strangers if you do this correctly.

How?

Perhaps the best way is to gain a following on social media by producing insightful content. You could start by creating a YouTube channel or starting a podcast. For those looking for a less intensive approach, becoming highly active on a platform such as LinkedIn could also gain you a significant number of followers. Other options might be Facebook, Reddit, Quora, or X (formerly Twitter)—depending on your industry or niche.

Putting yourself in the spotlight takes a strong dose of courage and a significant amount of work and effort (usually above and beyond your day job). If you highly value personal privacy, it may not be a comfortable choice. However, the payoffs can be significant. If you deliver quality insights, your audience will inevitably grow and people will subscribe to your content.

Best-case scenario, you could become a minor celebrity within your niche or industry. The demand for your products, services, and expertise could exponentially grow, as people in your industry will instantly recognize you and trust you as an authority.

The more likely scenario (and what I have seen and experienced personally) is your online content becomes a legitimate lead source. You may not become a minor celebrity, but people discover your material online (whether by accident or because they're searching for information), and they reach out. Once the dialogue starts, there's already a level of credibility baked in.

I would argue if you're not active on any of the social platforms, you're probably best suited for a career that doesn't involve B2B sales. While it's not inherently required to be actively engaged in social media, the lack of any presence on any platform puts you at a disadvantage in many cases. People are curious, particularly when they're researching where to spend their money.

CHAPTER 6

Microstories

How does one go about presenting evidence, facts, and figures in a sales presentation?

Before we dive deep to answer that question, let's fly up to thirty thousand feet for a moment.

How Retellable Is Your Sales Pitch?

When it comes to selling and presenting, there's one factor that's incredibly important and not often considered. How retellable is your pitch? Can the person (or people) who hear your presentation remember it, then turn around and retell it? Will they remember the core ideas of your presentation hours, days, or weeks later?

In B2B sales, the important purchasing decisions usually don't happen with the salesperson in the room. They happen behind closed doors, after the presentation or call.

It might be a front-line manager who really needs what you're selling but must convince the CFO before securing funds.

It might be a vice president who has the budget but must carefully navigate the internal politics with the procurement team.

It might be a product manager who is convinced your solution is a perfect fit but is debating other decision-makers who favor your competitor.

Whatever the case, chances are, you won't be in the room.

So how "retellable" is your pitch?

If there are too many facts, figures, stats, and technical details, your pitch won't be easily remembered.

Even seasoned presenters and veteran sales professionals have a major problem with including too much material in their slide deck. Generally everything goes: Sometimes a deck gets put together with dozens of complicated slides—some with five to ten bullet points or more.

This is where a presentation can come off the rails.

If you've got too much data and too many statistics—you're setting yourself up for a bad delivery.[8] The temptation will be too great to just read through every slide. Even if you can quickly sum it up, your audience members will be distracted trying to read your slides as you present.

They won't remember, and they won't be able to effectively retell your presentation.

You Might Need Two Slide Decks

You may need to create two different slide decks when selling. The first is your presentation deck. It's simple and clean. It includes high-level information and some thought-provoking images and graphics. During your delivery, the images on the slide will prompt you as you walk through the various stories, details, and data.

Your second slide deck, often called the *leave-behind slide deck*, resembles the first, but it's loaded with more information, bulleted items, and technical data. It's the slide deck that you email to your point of contact after the meeting.

What if the buyer (or the group listening to your presentation) is in the research phase of the Buyer's Journey? Aren't they looking for stats and information?

Yes, but it's how you deliver them that makes all the difference.

First, the good news: You've recognized where the prospect is in the Buyer's Journey. This will help you plan your presentation. You'll be better prepared with more information and details.

Still, you should resist the temptation to load your presentation deck with too much technical data—even when buyers are thirsty for information, as you can quickly drown them with too many bullet points and small fonts.

The key is knowing how to present details, facts, and features. This is not something accomplished with bulleted lists in a presentation. Just as you might convert fractions into decimals when doing arithemtic - when presenting you must learn to convert facts and figures into simple stories. You must also learn to skillfully ask the right questions to direct the narrative. Let's dive into both topics:

Using Microstories

The word *story* evokes the wrong thoughts and emotions as it relates to selling. When people think of the word *story*, their mind usually—whether consciously or unconsciously—goes to a place and time when they're sitting around a campfire or listening to a bedtime story while sitting on Grandpa's knee. Stories come in a wide variety of shapes, sizes, and colors. However, usually, when the topic comes up, people don't intuitively think about business stories in the world of sales and marketing.

The truth of the matter is stories are the delivery mechanism for facts, stats, and otherwise boring evidence and information. I'm a believer that for every significant fact or feature you have in your presentation, there should be a story to back it up.

Sounds like you need to know a lot of stories!

These stories also need to be memorized and rehearsed, and they should flow and be conversational. They need to sound natural and unscripted.

When I'm training professionals, most of them are relieved to learn these are not your normal stories. I'm talking about *microstories*.

Microstories are usually between twenty seconds and sixty seconds long. Stories don't always need a full narrative, with a cast of characters—often they're short anecdotes, simple analogies, or brief examples. They're microstories that you can quickly learn, practice with ease, and deliver naturally.

The Microwave Anecdote

One of my favorite microstories is an anecdote that I call the Microwave. I often use it when discussing the most important and necessary features of a given product and why a buyer may not need a feature they're asking about. It goes something like this:

"Think of a microwave. My microwave has twenty buttons. Guess how many I use? Two. I use the popcorn button, and I use the 'plus thirty seconds' button. That's pretty much it."

I will then tie together the analogy with the product I'm selling:

"This product does a few things really well but doesn't have that exact feature. How often do you use that functionality?"

Altogether, this microstory takes about twenty seconds to tell. It's a quick analogy that illustrates a point. It must be used at the right time and with the right tone, but it's effective, and everyone who hears it immediately understands.

Building a Catalog of Microstories and Anecdotes

The best practice is to keep track of your stories. It's not hard to keep a spreadsheet or a document where you write them down and sort them according to category or situation. If you've never done this before, you'll be surprised at how quickly your story collection will grow. This is where it can be a real advantage to practice your presentation with your colleagues. As you walk through your presentation, you'll share ideas and build off one another. It can become a fun exercise to swap stories, formulate analogies, and share examples when you have a small group practicing together—particularly when everyone has real experience and industry knowledge.

Zooming In and Out

One important factor with telling microstories is the ability to zoom in and zoom out. Specifically, this means being able to tell a short version, a mid-length version, and a longer version.

Start with a zoomed-out version. Can you tell the story in twenty to thirty seconds? You'll have to remove all but the most necessary points.

Here's a real example from my own career:

"There was a company based near Düsseldorf, Germany, that reached out to us. The CEO had this crazy idea for a simulator. Our team immediately knew his idea was neither practical nor possible, considering their budget. We came up with a ballpark price for his concept: € 2.8 million. I then flew to Germany to meet with him. He nearly choked when I told him the price. Then I showed him our most popular product, which had 90 percent of the features he wanted and only cost € 700,000. We ended up working together."

This microstory can be told in about thirty to forty-five seconds. However, I've found the Goldilocks version of this story is usually about two to three minutes long. This allows me to add some detail and context. If needed, I could easily turn this into a ten-minute story where I could talk about the CEO and discuss his situation in greater depth. I would then explain why his concept was flawed and what factors contribute to the cost of a custom simulation project. There's plenty of background and color I can add to this story.

The key is knowing the story well enough to deliver whichever version the situation requires, and have it feel unscripted and natural. Being able to read the room and adjust on the fly is necessary.

Simple is Best

When you're delivering stats or data, it can make sense to show a graph or chart to illustrate your point. Avoid the temptation to include too much when building out your slide deck. A complicated infographic that may be suitable for social media does not often work well for a presentation.

Simple is best. Remember that your PowerPoint slide deck is not your brochure. There's no need to have in-depth details, explanations, or a slide with multiple charts and graphics. Include one chart or one graphic to make your point, and then move on to a microstory or question.

There may be some situations where you need to show multiple different graphics that overlay data on a chart (perhaps to compare and contrast). Be sure to tread lightly. This type of analysis can be extremely useful, but it usually comes with fast-diminishing returns. Your audience will likely lose interest quickly.

As a general rule, it's better to have more PowerPoint slides with simple data and illustrations as opposed to fewer slides that have complex data, illustrations, and images. A complex slide or infographic triggers audience members to stop listening so they can read and analyze what's being shown to them on a screen. Slides and graphics should be ancillary, not integral to your presentation. Save the details and content for your "leave-behind" slide deck.

Memorize Your Material

When you're presenting data and stats, it's hugely advantageous to have practiced and memorized your material. The image or graphic should only be a queue that instigates the point you're trying to make and the associated story and follow-up questions.

Too often, sales professionals throw together a slide deck at the last minute, and the slide includes technical details that aren't memorized or practiced. The tendency for the presenter is to look back at the slide and read off the information displayed. This is the way the majority of people deliver their presentations.

However, there's a huge missed opportunity by doing things the same way as most presenters—first you miss out on a chance to build an enormous amount of credibility with your audience. By memorizing a few stats and delivering your material while facing your audience (not looking back at the display), you'll come across as competent and polished. Having mastery over your material is an easy way to build up credibility.

Additionally, as a presenter, you want to face the audience and detect their reactions and receptiveness to your content as you deliver the important points during your presentation. Reading the room will help you detect whether to zoom in or out on a specific point or story. This is difficult to do if you're paying too much attention to your slide deck or your notes.

The Conundrum with Discovery Questions

Asking the right questions during the sales process is especially important. Entire sales methodologies and sales coaching programs focus on asking a series of questions. Many of them have some excellent strategies and advice.

The problem that's not often addressed is that the buyer and seller often have the exact opposite intentions.

First, consider the situation. When do questions get asked? Presumably it's during a meeting or a Zoom call. But who set up the meeting? Under what pretenses? How long is this meeting, and what are the expectations?

Sometimes, just to get the meeting, the seller may have to agree to give up something (information, specifications, price).

There are instances when a potential buyer is willing to meet and be probed by a salesperson who is conducting discovery and diagnosing their pains and problems. However, even in the most favorable circumstances, there's usually a limit to how much structured interrogation the buyer is willing to endure.

Only a naive seller thinks they're going to have an hour or more to pepper the buyer with a series of SPIN questions in consecutive order.

This is why it's helpful to know where the buyer is along the Buyer's Journey ARC.

Most likely, if the buyer has instigated the meeting, they are in the research phase of the Buyer's Journey—meaning they're hungry for information and details.

Even if the buyer is in the awareness phase of the Buyer's Journey and has accepted a meeting out of courtesy and/ or curiosity, their expectation will still be to learn and gain insight from the interaction.

In either case, the buyer doesn't want an interrogation. A seller can quickly lose credibility and come across as inauthentic and salesy if they probe too much, too fast, or too deep with discovery questions. Trust must be earned.

On the other side is the seller.

The salesperson wants and needs the prospective buyer to open up. In a perfect world, they would like to ask all types of questions and learn everything they can early in the process. The more a seller knows and the earlier they know it, the better their chances.

What you have is a little conundrum. Both sides want information from the other side. The buyer is in the research phase and thirsty for facts and information. The seller wants to ask discovery questions before disclosing much information. How this information exchange plays out may determine if an opportunity stalls or turns into a legitimate deal.

Asking Questions Is Like Dancing

I was once in Buenos Aires on an extended business trip. As I don't frequently visit Argentina, I arranged my meetings so I could spend the weekend exploring the city. Over the course of the weekend, I enjoyed the sights and sounds of Buenos Aires by visiting the Teatro Colón and indulging in a succulent Argentinian steak. During my stay, I thought it might be fun to have a "when in Rome" experience by learning the Argentine tango.

While searching online, I found a place that taught tango lessons on the outskirts of downtown. I showed up the next evening at a dance hall where an instructor was teaching a group of about fifty people. I happened to be the only tourist in attendance that evening. It was the perfect atmosphere to learn the tango—a vintage building, dim lights, Argentinian music playing, and there was even an enormous mural of Eva Perón on the wall.

I stayed in the back and observed for a little while before mustering up the courage to join the main group. Initially the instructor showed us the steps as we followed along. Soon, we each paired off to practice the Baldosa (short basic step) with a dance partner.

I quickly gained confidence dancing in a curated environment and leading my partner in a novice variation of the tango. It was a fun experience. I led with each step, and my partner followed. Together we developed familiarity and rhythm, and we danced and learned from the instructor for about half an hour.

Tango is a dance that can be learned on a very basic level—but it's also an art that is mastered over many years. Once the very basic steps are learned, different variations are added; swivels, kicks, flicks, and other moves are inserted along the way.

Later in the evening, I had a truly embarrassing moment where I quickly learned just how complex the Argentine tango could be.

After an hour or so, the instructor-led portion of the evening ended—but the tango dancing continued as couples went out on the floor to practice their moves. As the night went on, more people came into the venue, some of them highly skilled dancers.

I made the mistake of observing from the sidelines too close for too long. Soon, a well-dressed young lady—who I did not recognize from my earlier class—grabbed my hand and pulled me onto the dance floor. I was initially shocked but thought to myself, "How hard can this be?" as I clasped her hand and started into the Baldosa I had just learned.

In less than ten seconds I realized I was out of my league. This gal was highly skilled and immediately tried some kind of twist move that completely threw me off. Complicating matters, she didn't realize I was a foreigner, and I couldn't understand much of her Spanish. I tried to restart at one point, but this only made matters worse. Soon she wanted me to follow her lead, but things unraveled pretty quickly. Altogether, it lasted less than ninety seconds before she gracefully dispatched me back to the sidelines and snatched a far more handsome and skilled Argentinian fella to match her talents in the tango.

While this is an amusing, if not embarrassing, story, I want to draw some parallels between dancing and asking questions in a sales environment.

When dancing the tango, there's a certain pattern, as someone leads, and the other person follows in their steps. If correctly done, there's a cadence and familiarity that develops, and the dance becomes easier and more natural for both dancers.

Asking questions in a sales environment can and should be like the tango. There's a cadence that occurs. The salesperson asks a question and then must wait for the buyer to respond before proceeding to the next question.

A rookie sales professional moves forward asking more memorized questions in a row, whereas a seasoned seller listens and responds with follow-up and drill-down questions such as "tell me more" or a mirroring question (where the seller repeats the few words of the buyer's answer with an upward inflection).

The key to all of this is to make sure the conversation is natural and not awkward—something easier said than done.

Reciprocity in Conversation

One way a sales conversation can become awkward or salesy is when the conversation feels more like an interrogation. Remember, we're dealing with the discovery conundrum. The buyer seeks information and insights. If the seller is only asking questions and probing while not providing information in return, the conversation won't seem natural, and the buyer will hesitate.

To avoid this, a seller must learn to share useful information and insights during the process. Here's one way to do it:

1. Start with a Microstory

2. Share an important and meaningful fact or statistic (immediately following the microstory)

3. Ask a relevant question.

With this approach, the buyer will start to feel like their gaining something from the interaction. Soon, they'll start responding with more lengthy and genuine answers. They may even reciprocate the pattern by sharing stories, meaningful facts, and asking questions of their own.

This type of back-and-forth cadence is far preferable (and more natural in conversation) than the interrogative approach some sellers will engage.

What Are the Best Questions to Ask?

The questions you ask in a sales situation may depend on your industry, the purpose of the meeting, and your objectives.

BANT Questions

Many sales organizations use a qualification framework called BANT. This is an acronym for *budget, authority, need, timeline.*

The BANT Framework has been around for decades. Some sales organizations adhere strictly to this framework when qualifying a buyer early in the sales process. Here are some examples:

1. Budget: What is the budget you have for this product/ service?

2. Authority: Who has the authority to make the final purchasing decision?

3. Need: Why is the product/service needed?

4. Timeline: What is the timeline for purchasing this product/service?

From the seller's point of view, BANT questions are terrific. They gather critical information that can help assess how serious a buyer is and where they are in the Buyer's Journey. The problem with BANT: it's outdated and one-sided. The seller gains all of the insight, and the buyer doesn't get much in return. These questions don't always lay the best foundation for a productive sales discussion.[9]

Additionally, sellers must be careful using BANT questions, as they can come across as very salesy. Asking a buyer about the budget and who has the authority to make purchasing decisions can be tricky.

In the case of an inbound lead, some of these questions may be asked to qualify—but a seller is not always working with an inbound lead.

I've found it's necessary to have a solid grasp of these questions—but to ask them with some discretion. There's no denying the importance of gaining knowledge of the buyer's budget, authority, need, and timeline. The key is knowing when to ask these questions.

Generally, it may not be best to lead with BANT questions. There's typically a better framework that leads to more productive sales conversations. BANT questions do need to be asked and answered, but think of them more as the supporting cast than the lead actors.

GAP Questions

There are two questions that can almost universally be used in most sales situations. If nothing else, knowing these two questions and framing them appropriately can set you up for success, regardless of the industry or product you sell:

1. **What product have you been using?**

This question can be tweaked and asked in a variety of different ways depending on the situation:

- What product have you used in the past?

- What service is your company using now?

- How has your company done this before?

Or you can ask more specifically about a product or vendor:

- Correct me if I'm wrong, but don't you guys have XYZ product?

- Doesn't your company use XYZ as a provider?

This is one of my favorite questions early in the sales cycle, as it's usually non-confrontational and easy for a buyer to answer. In most situations it opens up the opportunity for all sorts of follow-up questions while simultaneously providing insight into the buyer's situation. From here you can drill down and learn the situation, understand the buyer's motivations, discover problems, probe the pain points, and so much more.

If you're an adherent of *SPIN Selling* (famous book authored in the 1980s and used for decades by sales trainers), this question is a gateway for situation and problem questions, which can flow very naturally once the buyer opens up about what they've done in the past.

2. **What does your ideal situation look like?**

This question may take on various forms, such as follows:

- What product do you envision?

- What does the situation look like after you've made the acquisition?

- What is the perfect product for you?

- How does this play out if things go right?

- Where do you want to be?

The beauty of this question is that it bookends the previous question. We've previously found out where the buyer has been, and now we find out where they want to go. You've created a gap, as defined by the popular methodology Gap Selling[10], by uncovering the current state of the customer versus the desired future state. Once you've identified this Gap for the buyer, selling becomes more straightforward.

In the world of SPIN selling, this type of question is the gateway to implication and need—payoff questions— particularly as buyers start to put numbers and stats behind their current state versus desired future state:

"If you can solve this problem with X product and save Y amount of money, what would that mean to your company in terms of Z?"

Curiosity Questions

- In a previous chapter, we discussed likability, authenticity, and tone. It's a given here that your questions must be asked with a genuine and curious voice. As you proceed in this back-and-forth dance with the customer, asking questions and listening for answers, there are a few statements or prefixes that can help frame sales questions in a more humble and inquisitive tone that's likely to land better with the prospective customer.

  Here are a few examples:

- **"Help me understand..."** This quick statement works excellently as a prefix to almost any question. It conveys interest, curiosity, and even a certain amount of humility.

- **"Give me an example of..."** Asking for an example of a situation that a prospective buyer has just explained can provide you with clarity while telegraphing your interest and curiosity to the customer.

- **"Can you expand on that?"** This is just a drill-down question, but great for getting the prospect to open up on a specific issue. It also conveys curiosity.

In this chapter, one might feel I've meandered from the original topic of presenting facts and figures. The truth is, I haven't really meandered much at all. The big takeaway here is that when presenting facts and figures, less is better. Sales professionals should be judicious and selective when building their slide deck—using stats and evidence sparingly.

When you are presenting facts and figures, use microstories and practice using examples and anecdotes that can be told in seconds or expanded upon when needed.

Last of all, when you're delivering information and data, use the opportunity to ask insightful questions. Keep in mind, there's a balance. The buyer can drown in too much data—you'll bore people to death if your slide deck is full of stats, numbers, and evidence.

At the same time, a buyer can die of thirst if you withhold too much or only ask probing questions during your call or meeting. You need to find balance and engage in a dance with the buyer by giving and receiving information.

CHAPTER 7

Emotional **Selling**

Do People Buy Based on Emotion?

There's an adage in the world of sales that states:

"People buy based on emotion, then justify with logic."

This statement is true, but it's more complicated than most people realize.

First, we must ask some questions

- What industry are we discussing?

- What product are we selling?

- What specific emotion are we trying to evoke?

Perhaps most important:

- Are there effective strategies for selling with emotion?"

In most retail settings or situations where the transaction value is low and the stakes are small, raw emotion drives decisions, as the buyer speeds through the Buyer's Journey ARC very quickly.

Imagine choosing between a steak or a pasta dish at a restaurant—the decision is made in minutes (or even seconds) and is usually an emotional one to satisfy a craving.

Sometimes a decision is made as a response to fear—in many cases, the fear of missing out. "That sweater is 30 percent off right now with the holiday sale." SOLD!

Now, move up the spectrum to a B2B environment. Imagine a team of decision-makers evaluating the purchase of some capital equipment. The cost is hundreds of thousands of dollars, and the group will make a selection between vendors over the course of four to six months. In this situation, one might assume the decision is made based on logic—but this is not entirely true. Even in a complex enterprise B2B sales environment, decisions are still based on emotion.[11]

This is not to say that in a B2B situation the buyer will make a rash decision. Most likely, they'll be more cerebral and conduct some due diligence along the way. But in the end—the decision-makers are still humans, not robots. They still make up their mind based on feelings and impressions.

What Stories Really Sell?

In the last chapter, I wrote about microstories and how to use them to present facts, evidence, and details, rather than just drowning your prospects with raw data.

Stories have the ability to evoke emotion, but some stories can have more impact than others.

What are the best stories to tell to influence a buyer?

The best stories that have the most impact are not the stories we tell, but the stories told from the perspective of the customer.

Customer testimonials can move the needle far more than almost any story a salesperson can deliver. In an ideal situation, a customer testimonial can be delivered face-to-face or through a referral call - but that's not always feasible.

Video testimonials can be very effective- particularly if they can be used on demand in a sales situation. Years ago, this was a difficult proposition, as few companies took the time required to produce meaningful promotional videos and customer testimonials. Today, we live in the era of YouTube, TikTok, Instagram and more. A video testimonial is no longer a difficult proposition—it's table stakes.

If you're selling in a B2B environment, ideally you have a portfolio of video testimonials ready to use at your discretion.

In retail and transactional selling, we look for this type of social proof all the time. It's almost rare that we make a significant purchasing decision without first checking out the rating on Amazon or searching on YouTube for a video review.

In B2B selling it's really no different—studies show B2B buyers are online researching well before contacting a company to make a purchase.

Of course, there will be instances where you can't rely on a customer testimonial. Many times, when you're conversing directly with a prospective buyer, whether on a call or in a face-to-face meeting, the situation and logistics of showing a video can be inconvenient. Nevertheless, a good salesperson should still be able to tell a story from the customer's perspective by paraphrasing their sentiments.

Sell Through the Eyes of the Love Group

Years ago, during my master's degree program, I learned a great lesson about telling stories in sales situations from esteemed professor Michael Swenson at Brigham Young University. This lesson is noteworthy because it's applicable and easy to understand.

It assumes everyone you encounter in a sales or marketing situation falls into one of three different groups:

1.   The *hate group* are people who will never buy from you.

2. The *love group* are people who love what you sell. Presumably, these are mostly your existing customers.

3. The *swing group* are those in the middle. Most often, these are the people you'll be engaging with in a sales situation. They may not "love" what you sell (not yet anyway), but it's under consideration.

Here's the lesson: Market and sell to the *swing* group through the eyes of the *love* group.

Before you tell a sales story, perhaps you need to hear it first. Rather than speculating or guessing, it's usually best to just go interview those in the existing love group and hear their words firsthand. These are your brand advocates - they have the deep knowledge and can speak with emotion about your company and product. As you interview them, ask why they chose your company. What was their rationale? Find out about their buying experience and the research they did before making a purchase.

Too often, sales professionals are so engaged in prospecting and outreach that they forget the importance of gaining insight from existing clients. A sales story is so much more powerful if you can deliver it with conviction and quote first-hand the actual words spoken by those in your love group. You'll also gain confidence and motivation hearing these stories. The positive impact this will have on your own sales pitch could be significant.

The Power of Demonstration

As powerful as a story might be, don't assume an excellent story will instantly win over a customer. It could take much more. Remember, your competitors likely have stories of their own that they've repeated to the prospect. There's a chance that your amazing stories combined with excellent presentation skills are just barely keeping you in the hunt. If you really want to win over customers, you need more than a good story: you need emotional skin in the game.

The term *skin in the game* usually refers to when a person invests their resources into something (oftentimes a business or venture). The implication is that with skin in the game, someone is more committed and willing to stick it out when times get tough.

So how do you get a prospective buyer to have skin in the game? You do this through demonstration. Whatever you sell, do everything possible to let the buyer experience your product or service. Nothing comes closer to emotional commitment than a trial version or a demonstration where the prospective customer can experience the product in the flesh.

Whatever your industry, make sure there's a trial version, a tester, a sample, a sandbox version, or a demonstration available and ready for the buyer to experience. Allow the customer to partake, even if what you have to offer is very small or brief. This is how the prospect gets emotional skin in the game!

In my line of work (selling simulators), we will literally go to the ends of the earth to showcase our product in a face-to-face meeting for a prospective customer. As a premium provider, we know our product is more expensive than the competition. We also know if a prospective customer can properly test and experience our technology firsthand , we have a nearly 80 percent chance of winning the deal.

In 2019 we helped fly one potential client from New Zealand to Belgium so they could see and experiment with the very type of product they wanted. The cost was many thousands of dollars, but it allowed us to win a deal worth hundreds of thousands of dollars. Don't step over dollars to pick up nickels! Be generous and liberal with your samples, trials, and offers—especially when there's so much to gain in the long run.

Remember, you want to create a visceral connection with the buyer and your product (or service). They need to see themselves using your product. They need to envision doing business with you.

A friend in the residential real estate business once told me, "You know someone is close to making an offer on a home when they start talking about how to arrange the furniture in each room."

This statement rings true. You as the seller should encourage the client to envision the end state and help feed that conversation—whether in real estate or any other industry.

The Battle of Gut Feeling

There is one more emotion that should be written about—maybe the most important emotion when it comes to selling. This emotion is what is referred to as a *gut feeling*.

When somebody refers to *gut feel* or *gut feeling*, they're usually not talking about the product or features—but instead the company and/or the salesperson.

Turns out, a lot of B2B deals come down to gut feeling—research shows this may be as high as 84%.[12]

When the dollar values are high and the stakes are large with multiple competing parties, there's often not much differentiation between vendors.[13] It's a battle of excellent versus terrific. So who wins?

In this case, the client usually decides based on the mysterious gut feeling.

Just what is gut feeling? Is there any way to quantify it? In a competitive selling environment, how do we win the battle of gut feeling?

It turns out that the very actions we take early in the Buyer's Journey to build credibility and trust when the buyer is in the awareness phase are the very same actions that will help us win the battle of gut feeling as the deal culminates in a decision. We've come full circle!

To refresh your memory . . .

- Be competent.
- Be reliable.
- Be likable.
- Be authentic.
- Be confident.

There is also one other point to make...

Longevity Leads to Bluebirds

Longevity matters. Staying with the same company for several years can really compound your success in sales. The more you're a known quantity, the more prospective clients see you at industry conferences and events, the greater your likelihood of winning the battle of gut feeling.

This is a big reason why you may consider sticking with your current company rather than jumping from job to job (unless it's an offer you can't refuse). Selling becomes easier as you have more tenure in your current position. It's easier to win the battle of gut feeling when you've been around the block a few times.

If you really want to take this to the next level, be proactive in seeking out speaking engagements at industry conferences. Get yourself quoted in industry publications and newsletters. It's extra work—but it can lead to big dividends.

It turns out, there's a secret behind "bluebird" deals. They're rarely out of the blue. Usually, they come to those with more longevity—often from an introduction or impression made years earlier. The timing may have been wrong then, but now the prospective buyer is ready. Multiply this dozens (or even hundreds) of times over the course of many years, and you begin to understand the power of compounding in sales. Bluebird for the win!

CHAPTER 8

Slide Deck
Stratagies

It's time to pull together your presentation, dial in your pitch. Thus far you've learned a lot about the Buyer's Journey, about the importance of credibility, telling stories, asking questions, winning the battle of the gut feeling and more. This chapter reads more like a lighting round and covers some details to help you pull together your slide deck and prepare your sales presentation.

Remember—your sales pitch will vary depending on your audience, industry, setting, and more. Some of the tips presented here are better suited for presenting to a small group, and some are perhaps better when speaking to a large audience in a more general forum (similar to the scenario I described in the introduction to this book). Treat each of these as best practices and useful tips—not as strict canon. It's critical to learn how to tweak and customize your presentation to suit your audience.

Define Your Objective

What's the purpose of your presentation? Are you trying to sell something at its conclusion? Are you using it to set up your next meeting or get the prospective buyer to make a commitment? If you're presenting to a large group, your objective is likely to help educate your audience or gain exposure. Before you begin building out your slide deck or even preparing a script, start by defining your objective in one simple sentence.

Identify Your Audience

Who is your audience? Where are they in the Buyer's Journey? Are you presenting to a group of people who are already familiar with your company and product? Did they reach out to you and schedule the meeting? Chances are good they're in the research phase of the Buyer's Journey. If you're speaking at a large conference, your audience is almost certainly in the awareness phase of the Buyer's Journey. Identify where your audience is in the Buyer's Journey, and then move on to the next step . . .

Match the Method of Persuasion

Now that you've identified where your audience is in the Buyer's Journey, match the appropriate method of persuasion (as outlined in chapter 3). This is critical because it helps frame the entire presentation. It gives us a theme from which we can craft and develop messaging. If you're presenting to a group in the awareness phase of the Buyer's Journey, your focus should be on building credibility. When presenting to a prospective buyer in the research phase, you should be prepared to share evidence and thorough knowledge. If they're in the choice phase, focus on emotional "skin in the game," as discussed in chapter 7.

Start Bold

Your presentation needs to start strong. You need to share a story, throw out an alarming statistic, deliver an insightful (or attention-grabbing) quotation, give a mini demonstration, or conduct some sort of object lesson in the first thirty to sixty seconds. This should be polished and practiced and (preferably) lead into the core of your presentation. The last thing you want is to lose your audience just as you begin. Don't waste time with pleasantries such as, "So good to be here," or, "Thank you for allowing me to come." These pleasantries are meaningless and eat up valuable time that should be used to capture the attention of your audience. Aim to have your audience hooked in the first minute (or less).

If you're looking for an idea or story to begin your presentation in a bold fashion, one technique is to tell a brief story where you made a mistake or an error. It's been said that the most personal content is the most relatable, and tales of failure, danger, and disaster (when told authentically) hasten the deepest engagement.[14] Stories (similar to the story I shared as a young shoe salesman earlier in this book) can be great introductions, as they capture your audience while also allowing you to frame the rest of your presentation by sharing the valuable lesson learned from the mistake or embarrassment. This is surely not the only way to begin a presentation but just one idea that can work, depending upon your circumstances.

How Will You Be Introduced?

You must consider how you're being introduced to your audience or prospective buyers. In many cases, there may not be a need for an introduction, as it could be a follow-up visit with the same person or group(s). But often, there are new people in the room—different decision-makers or influencers who may not be familiar with you, the organization you represent, or your objective. For the sake of establishing credibility, you need to be introduced properly. A proper introduction means that you're present when the introduction occurs. Ideally the meeting host or emcee gives the introduction—this is usually the case when you speak to a larger audience. However, in many situations, you'll need to introduce yourself by giving a brief background of who you are, why you're there, and why they should believe what you say.

However, there's a problem with introductions: They're generally boring and can get in the way of starting bold, which we already established as extremely important.

Typically, I recommend jumping right into a story to capture and hook your audience. After your opening, whether it be a story, anecdote, quotation, or statistic, there's usually a brief opportunity to introduce yourself or reframe your introduction to establish your credibility.

I find in many cases, I'm introduced, but the introduction is very brief. I use the opportunity immediately following my opening to go into more depth on either my personal background or my company's background—whichever may feel more necessary and needed in the situation. Essentially, I shore up whatever might have been missed by the person giving the introduction.

Here's a situation that recently happened during a business trip. I walked into a pre-scheduled meeting in London. The setting was a large board room, and there were approximately ten people waiting for me in the room. This was my second meeting with this organization, as I had previously met with two of the senior managers who were in attendance. One of them welcomed me and introduced me to the rest of the group—but did so in a very brief manner (literally one sentence). I immediately jumped to my first slide, which included a curious picture and allowed me to give a brief (two-minute) story. This was my bold start. Once the story was complete, I had them hooked and had also gained a bit of credibility in their eyes (because my story included some industry-specific information). I then shared some more background information about me and my company (shoring up the introduction and giving the group a "reason to believe") before proceeding with the presentation.

3 High-Level Points

As you get into the core of your presentation, make sure you have only about three major points. Remember, the success of your presentation will largely depend on how well it is remembered by those in your audience and how well they can recall and re-pitch the presentation later to other colleagues and internal decision-makers. To maximize the opportunity for your presentation to be remembered, stick with three major points if at all possible.

Let's be real—most presentations will have far more than three points. You may have a variety of slides and pictures. You may plan to introduce a number of concepts. Your presentation may even be an hour long or more. How do you keep it to just three points? You might have to step back and try to organize your information under a certain theme. Can your three points relate to your company's core competency or the primary benefits of your product or service? Maybe it's an acronym. It could tie into a story or analogy. The key is to simplify the highest level of your message. Within the context of these key points, you can then include various bulleted items, details, pieces of evidence, slides, images, and more.

Structuring your content around three key principles has an added benefit—preparation becomes much easier as well. Rather than trying to memorize a list of fourteen key points, you can organize everything into segments that are easier to remember. The very practice of preparing your pitch and organizing into three key principles will help you dial in your narrative and theme. Ultimately your pitch will be more coherent.

Use the Opportunity + Solutions + Benefits Framework

If you're looking for content or trying to give structure to your presentation, consider using the Opportunity-Solution-Benefits Framework as discussed in detail in chapter 4. Using this approach will allow you to easily incorporate a story or an example (or a specific problem), showcase your company in a good light (providing a solution), and end with the benefits provided by the solution (which can evoke emotion).

Strongest Points First

As you create your deck and produce content for your presentation, start with your strongest point at the beginning. Just as your opening needs to be bold, as you get into the core of your presentation, start with your best content. If you're providing key points, start with your biggest and best. If you're giving a product demo, begin with the best feature. Presentations aren't like action movies or fireworks shows: You don't need to wait until the finale.

The chances of a meeting being interrupted, or a key decision-maker leaving early, or the Zoom call running into technical difficulties is just too great. Experts suggest that first impressions are so vitally important that you should always start with your best content.[15]

Build Your Leave-Behind Slide Deck

When creating a new slide deck for a presentation, start by building out your leave-behind slide deck. This is a content-heavy slide deck that may have many bulleted items and text-heavy information. It's the slide deck you'll leave behind with prospective customers after your presentation—giving them plenty of data, evidence, and statistics to consider. You're not going to present with this slide deck, but it's an excellent place to start and helps us ensure we've got all the right information included. It also helps us as we begin practicing our pitch. We'll become familiar with the content and order of the presentation, then look to trim out the details as we practice and get closer to delivering the presentation.

Connect Your Conclusion with Your Bold Start

The conclusion to your presentation should be relatively easy. If you've structured your presentation using some high-level points, your conclusion should summarize those points. A summary conclusion doesn't need to take longer than a minute or two—it can be very brief. Assuming the core of your presentation was well executed, a simple summary conclusion is a safe bet. But you might not be content with just a simple summary. If you really want to "stick the landing" and score a 10, you'll need to show some creativity.

If you started your presentation with a story, anecdote, or analogy, there's almost certainly an opportunity to finish your presentation with a concluding story that ties into your introduction. This is just one strategy, but there's usually an ending that you can withhold until your conclusion, or perhaps it's a different story that ties into the same concept you introduced early in your presentation. A good callback story is a terrific way to neatly wrap up your presentation. There are other strategies as well. If you've used an interesting quotation or statistic, there's almost certainly another that relates (perhaps the same author or the same statistic shown with new data). Look for a clever way to connect your intro and conclusion. A little brainstorming session may be required, but there's almost always a way to connect the beginning with the end.

Ask a Concluding Question

As you conclude, you should always be ready to ask a pivotal question of your audience at the end of the presentation. The question will largely depend upon your objective and where the buyer is in their journey. If you're selling something transactional (low dollar value), you might be bold and simply ask a direct closing question such as "What keeps you from purchasing XYZ product right now?" The key here is to be careful with your tone and try not to sound salesy. Best-case scenario, your prospect moves forward with the purchase—or (more likely) you learn their key objection(s).

If you're speaking with a large audience (perhaps at a conference) or with prospective buyers who are very early in the awareness phase of the Buyer's Journey, your concluding question might be more of a challenge, focused on getting them to connect with you or accept a discovery meeting.

In a B2B environment where you have a complex deal, the question should pertain to the next step in the process, which could be something like, "What information do we need to gather so I can send you a proposal?"

The key here is the concluding question should pertain directly to your original objective, which you outlined before you built out your slide deck.

How to Polish Your Presentation

Add Stories

This should be relatively easy to do once you have a first draft of your slide deck. You should have a variety of potential stories or microstories (chapter 6). Start to practice how and when in your presentation you'll deliver your stories. Determine which stories are critical and which can be reduced to a small microstory or eliminated altogether if necessary.

Add Questions

Now do the same with questions. Determine what questions will be important to ask prospective buyers during your presentation. They may be discovery questions, GAP questions, or other questions that help facilitate communication. Make sure the questions aren't too salesy, and begin to practice your tone. If you're presenting to a large audience, you may be asking very general rhetorical questions that won't necessarily evoke a response, but you can still ask (and sometimes answer) your own questions and seek confirmation from the larger group. Remember—if your presentation provides valuable insights and information to your audience (whether large or small), they'll likely reciprocate and provide you with insightful details in return.

Add Comedy

As your presentation is coming together, consider adding a dose of comedy to it. Your goal is not to be a standup comedian, but some light comedy or a funny, relevant story can certainly help you build rapport with prospective buyers. If you're speaking to a larger group, it will help you build a connection and endear you to the audience.

There are a few easy ways to add humor to your presentation. The rule of three is easy to learn and incorporate into your presentation. It's a simple list, a pattern, where the third item is nonsense or absurd. It's very easy to dream up quick punchlines.

Example: Last night for dinner I had ribeye steak, apple pie, and heartburn.

There are countless other ways to add comic relief to your presentation. Exaggerations, comparisons, observations, ironies, and even sound effects are good ways to evoke a little laughter.

I find that telling a self-deprecating story, where my foolishness or ignorance is on display, usually provides some comedic relief.

The key in a business or sales presentation is to not try too much or too hard. Stand-up comedians go for multiple laughs each minute. Your goal in a sales presentation is to maybe get a handful over the course of a thirty- to sixty-minute presentation.

Next, you will need to practice your delivery. Get comfortable telling a funny story or one-liner. How it lands will depend on a variety of factors, including your tone and the mood of your audience. What may work one day won't work the next with a different group. Once you gain some live experience, you can begin to dial in how some comedy will fit into your presentation.

Aesthetics

It's now time to clean up your slide deck. Make sure to have consistent fonts and double check the spelling and punctuation.

Most presentation experts suggest using a darker background for your slides. Generally colors such as blue, gray, and black provide a better viewing experience that's less stressful on the eyes. Darker colors (typically with light gray or white text) are easier to read when the room is dim. This is not a rule you must abide by 100 percent of the time, but it is a recommendation that seems to be common among experts. [16]

Have Your Social Media Ready

It's very likely that whether you're presenting to a small number of decision-makers or to a large audience, someone will be going online to visit your social media profiles. Be aware, they may visit more than your company's web page or your LinkedIn profile. People can be curious, and there's a chance they'll snoop around your personal Facebook page or Instagram account. They may deep dive into content you posted months or even years ago.

It's a very good idea to audit your social media to see what's available for public consumption and what's locked down. Keep in mind, if you're expecting people to trust and believe in the product or service you're selling, you should also expect those people to research you online. Don't act surprised when they find you even if you're a very private person.

I prefer a proactive approach. I invite people to visit my website and connect with me on LinkedIn. Usually, I do this as I conclude my presentation. It's easy to add a QR code, along with an email address, to the last slide of your presentation.

In reality if you're not asking people to connect with you, it's a missed opportunity! Remember, if you're presenting to a larger audience, most of them are likely in the awareness phase of the Buyer's Journey. They're not ready to buy yet, but they could be ready to follow you online. It's an easy ask, and if they do follow or connect, you're now on their radar. If you publish content proactively, you can begin to build up that reservoir of credibility. When the time comes, they'll likely seek you out, and you could be on your way to a bluebird deal!

CHAPTER 9

Delivering Your Presentation

Let's assume for a moment that you've already prepared your slide deck. Or perhaps you're in a situation where you don't need a slide deck—maybe you'll be delivering your pitch at a restaurant or on the golf course. In this chapter, similar to chapter 8, various different best practices are provided to help you polish the delivery of your sales presentation. It's likely some of these won't be applicable in your situation. That's OK. Remember, these are not hard rules, but recommendations to help you as you present, whether in front of a large audience, in a boardroom, or around a kitchen table.

Practice Makes Perfect

Don't practice with your prospective client! It happens to all of us: We spend 95 percent of our preparation time organizing the slide deck, and we have no time left to practice before our pitch. Don't let this happen. Your effectiveness will drastically improve with practice! Once you know the slide deck and content, the transitions become easier and the sentences flow better for both you and the audience. The result will be fewer "ums" and "ahs," and your stories will sound more natural. Your eye contact and body language will also improve.

If you're presenting in front of a large audience, such as giving a talk at a conference, you'll want to rehearse a minimum of five times before your presentation. Even if your presentation is more intimate, such as in a boardroom to a small number of people, practicing and role-playing will be extraordinarily helpful. It may even be worthwhile to set up a camera and take a video of yourself going through your presentation. It can be uncomfortable to see yourself on camera, but (in most cases) you'll become your own best critic and immediately spot some things to improve.

Pay close attention to your tone. Focus on removing any "salesy" language and tone from your presentation. Sometimes it's easier to detect a problem with your tone when you view a recording of yourself. The minimal trouble of setting up a camera and the awkwardness of watching your own rehearsal are absolutely worth it if you can iron out a few of your stories and correctly adjust your tone to minimize the salesy-ness of your pitch.

It's no secret that Steve Jobs was a legendary presenter. His introduction of both the iPod (2001) and iPhone (2007) were hugely impactful. These presentations can easily be found on YouTube, and they're worth watching, particularly if you want a trip down memory lane.

What's lesser known is that Steve Jobs was almost obsessed with practice and preparation ahead of these product launches.[17] He dialed in his pitch and began working on the delivery several weeks in advance, often scripting out each sentence. Your pitch may not change the world of technology in quite the same way as the introduction of the iPhone, but practicing ahead of time, especially when the stakes are high, will almost always pay off.

Remove the Data

Resist the temptation to leave detailed data on your slides. If you've practiced your presentation, there won't be a need to keep that stuff in your deck. Your slide deck should be images and maybe a few salient bullet points. Don't compete for attention with your slide deck! Your slide deck should contain so little data that it should be difficult for someone to follow the narrative without your commentary. Remember, you can always leave behind a different (more detailed) slide deck after your presentation.

Inspection Before Presentation

This point might be more salient when giving a sales presentation or speech to a larger group, but it's worth sharing, nonetheless. Make sure to inspect the venue before your presentation. Have a backup of your PowerPoint ready on a jump drive (in case of emergency). Make sure you're familiar with the slide clicker. (An unfamiliar slide clicker can be frustrating.) It's likely there's an audio/visual specialist that can assist you with a microphone check or even a dress rehearsal. One common problem that occurs is when your presentation includes a video with sound. Make sure the audio can be heard throughout the venue.

Body Language When Presenting

Before your presentation, you should have an idea of where you'll be standing. There's a good chance you'll be constrained by a podium or lectern. This is not ideal, but sometimes it is unavoidable. If you have a choice, it's best to be mic'd up and have the flexibility to walk around the stage. If you walk around, don't abuse it too much. Walking around can be distracting. Go with what feels natural.

If you're presenting to a small group, consider the sunrise-sunset body language rules (chapter 5). Avoid standing front and center. Consider positioning yourself toward the front of the room, in a diagonal position that allows you to face the individuals in the room but doesn't come across as too powerful or self-promoting.

Hand Gestures

Most communication and speaking professionals say it's best to avoid putting your hands in your pockets or fidgeting with your hands. If you're behind a lectern, avoid the temptation to lean on the lectern or even touch it all.

Focus on your hand gestures. Some of the best speakers use hand gestures to emphasize almost every sentence.[18] A good speech may even have hundreds of hand gestures, as the speaker has become natural and relaxed at just letting them go.

Too Loud Is Better than Too Soft

Many people tend to speak too softly during their presentation. Even when you're speaking into a microphone, make sure you have enough volume. Inexperienced presenters are often hesitant when they speak into a microphone as they hear their own voice reverberate through the sound system. It can be awkward if you're not used to it. Be careful! If your voice is too faint, it doesn't matter how well your content is structured or how many great stories you tell, your presentation will flop. You're better off being too loud than too quiet. Speak up!

If you're presenting in a smaller room to a group of less than ten, it's easier to gauge your volume. Where presenters often get into trouble is when they're speaking in a medium-sized room, such as a classroom. In some cases there may be thirty to forty people in the room and some ambient noise. In these situations, remember that you're better off being a little bit too loud rather than a little too soft. This is true with or without a microphone.

Remember to Slow Down

Studies show that over 80 percent of people will feel some level of anxiety or nervousness before delivering an important speech.[19] This nervousness causes most people to speak faster when they're in front of an audience, sometimes as much as 50 percent faster.

My teenage son was recently preparing a short five-minute memorized speech which was to be delivered in front of about two hundred people. I worked with him for several days on telling the stories and putting them to memory. The morning of his speech, he had it all ready to go, fully memorized and polished up nicely. I clocked him several times practicing his talk, including just an hour before his scheduled time to step up to the microphone. His speech was exactly five minutes, each and every time. Yet, once in front of the audience, adding a little nervousness to the environment, his five-minute speech took only three and a half minutes. He didn't miss a single word, nor did he catch his breath.

You may not be as nervous as a teenager in front of a large group, but chances are you'll be a little nervous before your presentation, and this nervousness will result in talking faster. Be aware that your last practice run will likely be a little better than your actual delivery. One good strategy is to plan a brief pause during a specific point in your speech. Or, ask the audience a rhetorical question. Find a way to slow your pace down if you have this tendency.

Eye Contact – Don't Look at the Display

Remember to maintain good eye contact with your audience. This shouldn't be too difficult for most sales professionals. However, if you're in front of a larger audience presenting in an auditorium or on a stage, be careful not to turn your back to the audience, presumably to look up at the screen. Also, avoid constantly looking straight down at the confidence display (the TV display that sits on the floor and allows the speaker to see what's on each slide). You should know your material well enough that you could present without your slide deck if necessary.

Don't Apologize or Make Excuses

Even if you're a skilled presenter, something will often go wrong during your presentation. It may be something simple—perhaps you forgot a story, mispronounced a name, included the wrong picture on a slide, or something else minor. Here's an important tip: Don't apologize! Unless you've made an egregious error, apologizing will only draw attention to your mistake and create an awkward situation. Simply move on. Those who may have noticed your error will most likely forget as you continue on with your presentation.

Similar to apologizing is making excuses. Among novice speakers, there's a tendency to announce the fact that they're inexperienced or nervous. This also draws attention away from the message. Whether new or experienced, there's usually no need to make any excuses. Stick with the content.

Over the course of my career, I've found that mishaps often happen during product demonstrations. Particularly when a complex piece of equipment or a feature-rich software product is being showcased, there's always a chance something won't work right.

Years ago, I was conducting a product demonstration with my business partner. An important client was visiting our headquarters and wanted to see a detailed demonstration of our latest technology. As I turned on the system, there was a glitch with the software. It occurred at just the wrong time, and I had to reboot the computer while everyone was waiting. The situation was a bit awkward, and my business partner offered an apology. Time continued to pass, and it was certainly a "hold your breath" moment for both of us, hoping the system would boot up correctly. My business partner soon offered another apology and then (a few moments later) a half-baked excuse. Yes, the situation was (for us) a bit tense, but (as I explained to my partner later) the apologies and excuses only made the situation worse by drawing attention to the problem. The entire sequence may have felt like a long time, but it was only about ninety seconds. Had we not brought any attention to the situation, the client may not have realized anything was out of sorts. Lucky for us, the system did boot correctly, and we moved on with our demonstration. As is usually the case, mishaps are often quickly forgotten unless you put a spotlight on them by over-apologizing.

It's Better to End Early

With almost every presentation, it's a good idea to end just a little bit early. Much the same way that it's best to be a little too loud with your voice rather than too soft when presenting, it's best to wrap up your presentation slightly ahead of expectations.

Going on too long can absolutely kill your presentation and unravel the goodwill you've built up. This is especially true if you're presenting to a larger audience (at a conference). Some people are very anxious about their time, especially if they're on a tight schedule and needing to get to the next session, or (even worse) desiring to get in line for lunch. I've seen so many presentations and speeches that have done everything right, but they failed to stick the landing because they went on too long.

Always end five to ten minutes early. Leave time for questions and networking. Don't risk going over on time!

CHAPTER 10

Closing
The **Deal**

The Truth about Closing a Deal

Much of this book, up until this chapter, has focused on communicating and presenting to potential buyers. We've learned numerous strategies on how to build credibility, how to tell stories, and how to ask questions, and even a few pointers on how to present to a large audience.

But how do you actually close a deal?

There's an idea in the world of sales that one must be a good closer to effectively sell. But what, exactly, does it mean to be a good closer?

Is it what Hollywood portrays?

In a famous scene from the 1992 movie *Glengarry Glen Ross*, a sharply dressed and highly successful sales leader named Blake, played by Alec Baldwin, excoriates a group of lazy sellers and introduces a concept to them—ABC (Always Be Closing).

This acronym, ABC (Always Be Closing) has become well known, even outside the world of sales. What exactly does it mean?

The funny thing is the movie never really explains. Alec Baldwin's character never gives us a real explanation or example. We don't get to see him close any sort of deal. That particular scene, while iconic in the world of sales, is mostly just a bunch of insults and bluster, coupled with some fantastic acting.

Somewhat ironically, written on the chalkboard during the scene, right next to Always Be Closing, is AIDA. This old marketing acronym is closely related to the Buyer's Journey ARC written about at length in chapter 1 of this book. Alec Baldwin's character glosses over AIDA during his monologue in a nonsensical manner. One of the core truths to effective selling was right there in plain sight for everyone to see, but not given the proper attention or context.

What about the 2013 movie *The Wolf of Wall Street*? In a famous scene, a silver-tongued phone salesman named Jordan Belfort (played by Leonardo DiCaprio) leaves his coworkers speechless by effortlessly persuading a guy over the phone to invest thousands of dollars in worthless penny stocks.

It's not too dissimilar from the 2000 movie *Boiler Room*, where a slick-talking character played by Vin Diesel schmoozes a wealthy doctor on a call by delivering some well-rehearsed lines.

Is closing that simple? If a salesperson learns to talk fast, memorizes a few good lines, and perfects their tone and delivery, can they effortlessly convince someone on a cold call to purchase a product even when they're (literally) selling junk?

The truth is many of these famous portrayals are pure fiction. They're showing fraudsters and con artists, not true sales professionals. These scenes may evoke an adrenaline-fueled fist pump and a favorable audience reaction, but trying to emulate or recreate these strategies in a real sales situation isn't likely to yield results and will probably do more harm than good.

Yet some of these ideas, like "Always Be Closing" persist.

Let's go beyond Hollywood portrayals.

In many real-life industries, usually where selling is more transactional, it's believed and taught by some sales leaders that one must learn closing strategies and techniques to convince a buyer to sign.

If you Google "closing techniques" you may come across a variety of tactics—many have been around for decades and have specific names:

- The assumptive close
- The alternative close

- The sharp angle close

- The Colombo close

- The puppy dog close

- The sales contest close

- The hard close

Do these actually work?

Be cautious! Most of these techniques are outdated and work by ramping up the pressure in a manipulative way. If you're using a tactic that is salesy or manipulative, it could damage your credibility, if not in the short term, certainly in the long run.

A wise instructor I had during my executive program at the Kellogg School of Management, Clinical Professor Craig Wortmann, said it best:

"Closing is the natural outcome of a sales process done well."[20]

I've found this to be very true in my own career. If you've fostered a good relationship, paid close attention to the buyer's experience, built up your credibility, shown competence, asked and answered the right questions, and done this all in a sincere and likable manner, closing a deal becomes almost inevitable. It's a natural outcome. In many cases the buyer may even initiate the closing. There's really no need to ramp up the pressure or learn any specific closing technique.

This is not to say you shouldn't ask for the business. Sometimes it will take a nudge. Often by asking a closing question, you can flush out any final objections or concerns. The way to do this is not through some manipulative or high-pressure technique. It's usually as simple as asking, "What's the next step?" or explaining the next step in the process and then asking for permission.

Being transparent during the sales process and communicative to the buyer on the next steps is always a highly effective strategy. It's quite possible (depending upon the industry) that the buyer is a novice buyer and doesn't know the proper steps to take when purchasing a product. An effective salesperson should shepherd the buyer through the process by continually pointing out the next steps, whether it be a demonstration, a proposal, an introduction, a technical review, terms and conditions, etc.

Perhaps it's best to rework the ABC acronym into something more useful than "Always Be Closing." A far better ABC acronym might be . . .

ABC – Always Be Curious

A sales professional should Always Be Curious. This applies when building a professional relationship with a prospective customer, learning about the needs and pains of the buyer, and handling any objections.

An integral part of working with a buyer is knowing where they are in the Buyer's Journey. Be curious about their viewpoints and the perspective from which they view the market.

Too often, as sellers, we get mired in the mud of our own sales processes. We're too busy trying to crank out proposals and moving opportunities from stage 2 to stage 3 to stage 4 in our sales pipeline. Instead, we need to get inside the buyer's mind and help mentor them along in the process. We need to listen to what buyers are saying about their journey and work on continually improving their experience.

Sales Methodologies

If you're a top-level sales professional and (especially) if you're leading a sales team, you've probably been curious about different sales methodologies that can better your results. There's no shortage of content on this topic. Chances are good you've already bought a book, listened to a podcast, or seen videos on YouTube relating to different sales methodologies. If you haven't already, you can always hire a consulting firm to implement a methodology and train your entire team. The real question is, which sales methodology is best?

I like to think about sales methodologies the same way I think about pizza. Think for a moment about the various types of pizza out in the world. Some of the most popular include the following:

- New York pizza

- Chicago deep dish

- Neapolitan

- Detroit style

Likewise, there are various types of popular sales methodologies, including the following:

- Challenger

- SPIN

- Sandler

- MEDDIC

How are sales methodologies and pizza alike? People can really get passionate about which style they prefer. Over the course of my career, I've researched and tried variations of most of them. There's some really good stuff out there! Quite frankly (just like pizza), I really love certain aspects of each.

As the head of sales and co-owner of a company, I get to decide which sales methods and processes we use. In our case, we sell high-ticket products to a niche market. Our industry and situation is unique; therefore, we've crafted our own recipe. It borrows a lot from Challenger and other methodologies. We also have our own special sauce—a unique framework that I developed (along with input from our team) that works exceptionally well for long sales cycles.

Over the course of my career, I've seen companies (large and small) achieve success using different sales processes and methodologies. Yes, I believe companies can have success by blindly adopting a sales methodology. However, most companies may need to tweak some things to align a methodology with their company's strategy, industry, and culture.

The method I created for our company is somewhat unique. It looks and smells a lot like the other pizza but tastes slightly different. We've been eating it for years and our team has bought into our methodology and processes (which is key). We all like it and adhere to it, and it's delivered excellent results.

CHAPTER 11

The **Get** vs. **Go** Framework

What is the "special sauce" we use at our company? When considering sales methodologies, I believe the definition gets a bit fuzzy, whether talking about a methodology, a sales strategy, sales skills, or best practices.

In our case, we use what I call the Get vs. Go Framework. It's a simple concept but helps define our strategy and is especially good when working with big-ticket items and with long sales cycles.

How Does Get vs. Go Work?

It's very simple: For each opportunity in our sales pipeline, we assign two scores:

The Get Score, measured from 1 to 100, is the probability that a prospective buyer chooses our company, if the decision were to be made today.

The Go Score, also measured from 1 to 100, is the probability that a prospective buyer will make a decision and sign a deal (whether with us or the competition) in the next ninety days.

Multiply both scores together (then divide by 100), and you have the Get vs. Go Total Score— which is the true probability of the deal closing.

Get vs. Go Examples

Here are some examples from my own company that may help clarify how Get vs. Go works. Naturally, you'll have to adjust and tweak for your own use.

Scenario #1

An account executive is working with a prospective buyer whom he met at a trade show last year. He's had several calls with the company, and his primary contact absolutely loves our product and has seen it demonstrated and used by another one of our customers. Unfortunately, the account executive was recently informed that the budget was not approved by the CFO. When our account executive was visiting the company a few months ago, he spent a considerable amount of time with the training and operations team, but only met briefly with the CFO, who was polite but did not ask any specific questions.

Get Score = 80	In this scenario, the account executive has built up a great relationship over several months with an internal champion who loves the product, as well as others within the organization. Several calls and an in-person meeting have occurred. It appears that someone is trying to obtain funds from corporate. We can assume if the budget were approved and this buyer was making the decision today, we would have an 80 percent chance of winning the deal.
Go Score = 30	There's little chance this deal will close in 90 days or less. The CFO doesn't seem engaged, and our account executive has just been informed the budget may take some time for approval. The Go score is on the lower end, but we'll be generous and give it a score of 30 because it seems there's a real effort to get budget approval.
Total = 80 × 30 / 100 = **24**	

Scenario #2

A different account executive has another prospective buyer in her funnel. This opportunity reached out via email a few weeks ago. The account executive has not met them in person. On a recent Zoom call, the buyer asked about the development time before the solution can be installed and also some specific questions about features that are prominent in the solution sold by our competitor. This buyer is price sensitive and urgent to get a proposal update. The account executive and a sales engineer already provided the buyer with a trial "sandbox" version of our software, but internal analytics show the buyer has only logged in a couple of times.

Get Score = 30	Several indicators hint that this prospective buyer is strongly considering the competitor's product. The fact that the buyer is asking about curious features and not using a trial version would certainly suggest that, if they were to make a purchasing decision today, they would likely go with a competitor. Yet, the buyer is still engaging (rather than ghosting). Possibly they're trying to get a competitive quote. 30 seems like the right score.
Go Score = 70	The customer seems anxious to get a proposal update (sometimes called a *best and final offer*) and is asking detailed questions about delivery time. These are indicators the buyer is getting close to making a decision. Since we don't absolutely know the time frame, we'll give it a score of 70.
Total = 30 x 70 / 100 = **21**	

Scenario #3

This company has been in the CRM system since they originally made an inquiry on our website two years ago. Over the last several months, the account executive has proposed a solution and has had good correspondence with this company. (They've been complementary about our product.) Six weeks ago, they reached out directly for technical details, as they're putting together the final requirements for an RFP (request for proposal). The account executive has arranged for an official demonstration of our product at their headquarters, which will occur in two weeks in front of a committee of executives and senior managers. Correspondence has been continual with the VP of operations and VP of finance, who has asked specific questions about payment terms and other contractual details.

Get Score = 90	Indicators look excellent with this opportunity. Correspondence has been going on for several months. The AE has been in direct contact with multiple decision-makers who are asking the right questions. Perhaps most importantly, they've reached out for product details to use in the requirements for their RFP. All indicators point to a high Get Score of 90.
Go Score = 80	As there is an official RFP, it appears a decision will occur in the next few weeks. While RFPs can occasionally be delayed or canceled, in this case, considering the questions and correspondence with the decision-makers, the Go Score seems very high.
Total = 90 × 80 / 100 = **72**	

Get Score Insights

At a high level, the Get Score is closely connected to the core principles of persuasion as learned in chapter 2. It's essentially a way to quantify whether or not we've established enough ethos (credibility), logos (logic), and pathos (emotion) with the buyer.

A buyer with a Get Score of 80 or 90 has usually given a strong verbal commitment or indication that they will be buying the product. A score around 50 suggests that the buyer is considering but is still up in the air regarding their decision, whereas a Get Score of 20–30 suggests the buyer is favoring the competition, meaning you're the underdog or you're one of several companies being considered and you don't have any clear advantage.

The Best Strategy to Raise the Get Score

A good place to start might be the topics discussed in chapter 6 of this book. Can you conduct a demonstration and try to appeal to the buyer's emotions? Are you selling through the eyes of the "Love Group" by telling impactful stories? Can you win the Battle of Gut Feeling? Also revisit the items from chapter 5, particularly with regards to asking the right questions. Oftentimes, late in the Buyer's Journey, the research and discovery phase has passed, but certain objections and concerns may have arisen. Keeping an open dialogue with the buyer (if it's not prohibited by RFP rules) can only be helpful.

Resist the temptation to lower the price. Yes, it can work in some instances to win a deal, and in some cases (particularly if you're an underdog or if it's a highly strategic account), it may be worthwhile. However, this should be used as a last resort. There are certain dangers (both short term and long term) to playing pricing games. Win by selling the value of your product, not by selling the value of your deal.

Years ago, I came upon an opportunity very late. The prospective customer was already close to signing with my competitor, and I was clearly the underdog. They also indicated their timeline for making a decision was very short. The Get Score would have been around 20, and the Go Score around 70.

I had to act fast, so I met with my partner, and together we came up with a plan. We agreed this particular company would be a highly strategic account for us to win, and as such, we would pull out all the stops. Our strategy was to offer a demonstration in Antwerp, Belgium, the site of our most loyal customer. I called up the buyer and informed them that (if they were willing) we would pay for their visit to Antwerp the following week, no questions asked. They were surprised by the generosity of the offer and decided to make the visit.

A few days later I met them in Antwerp, where they spent an afternoon trying out multiple systems and listening to the positive feedback of our best client. I then spent the next day escorting them to Bruges and nearby Amsterdam as we tasted chocolate and waffles and shared a few laughs. Meanwhile, along with building a strong personal connection, I was able to uncover and resolve some of their last-minute objections and concerns. A few weeks later I signed them to a seven-figure deal. The demonstration and personal testimonial from our client in Antwerp moved the needle from a Get Score of 20 to about 90. The chocolate and waffles made up for the rest.

Go Score Insights

Just as the Get Score is connected to the methods of persuasion from chapter 2, the Go Score correlates with the Buyer's Journey ARC that we learned back in chapter 1. It's a numerical measurement of where the buyer is along the ARC. As the buyer moves from awareness to research, their score goes up. Ultimately, as they approach a choice, the probability (score) gets closer and closer to 100.

The Go Score requires the salesperson (and others on the team) to think more in depth about the Buyer's Journey. Consider scenario #1 from earlier in this chapter. It's likely (at many organizations) that this type of deal would be categorized into a sales stage with a high probability of closing. With the Go Score considered, we're much more realistic about the deal's chances of closing and tuned into where the buyer is in their journey.

There also must be a timing factor incorporated into the Go Score, which, at our company, is ninety days. There can be some flexibility with the timing factor. You can adjust your Go Score depending on your industry and the length of the typical sales cycle. (Perhaps sixty or thirty days is better for some companies with shorter sales cycles.)

One interesting aspect of the Go Score is it doesn't take into consideration the expected closing date. This prevents an artificially high Go Score on a deal that's many months (or years) away. Even though virtually every CRM system requires a closing date, often it's just a guess–especially with longer sales cycles. Remember, the Go Score is simply the probability that a buyer will make a decision and sign a deal (whether with us or the competition) in the next ninety days. The nearsightedness of the Go Score keeps a sales team focused on the prospective buyers as they're making critical decisions.

As you consider the Go Score, it's also important for the buyer to be moving toward a choice, or else the score will decrease. An opportunity can (in theory) stay in the pipeline for a very long time, but the Go Score gives it some accountability. A good sales manager will continually question a sales professional about the Go Score. If nothing is happening, the Go Score will decrease regardless of how much the buyer favors us over the competition.

The Best Strategy to Raise the Go Score?

Patience and persistence are typically the best approach when a buyer has a high Get Score but a low Go Score. In many B2B situations, there may not be too many actions you can take to move the needle immediately. Think of the situation like a long tennis volley. Your best strategy is to not make any mistakes. You shouldn't ramp up the pressure when (it's likely) you're waiting for a budget to be approved or an RFP to be released. Creating false urgency is akin to hitting the tennis ball too hard and watching it sail out of bounds.

Likewise, you must continue to take action and engage with the buyer. Consistent follow-up and communication are key. Those who assume the deal will just eventually happen and neglect to follow up with the buyer are essentially hitting the ball into the net. Relationships must be maintained, and direct communication (from sales) and broader marketing efforts (email newsletters, promotions, etc.) should be ongoing.

Advantages of Get vs. Go

Prioritize Opportunities

The Get vs. Go allows a sales organization (including sales managers, account executives, and other stakeholders) to dive in and gain immediate insight on two critically important aspects of a prospective deal. Virtually all aspects associated with closing the deal are incorporated into either the Get Score or the Go Score.

In most cases, the account executive is providing both scores based on their best guess. However, they must be able to justify their score with specific details if (for instance) asked during a sales meeting. An effective sales manager can drill down by asking the salesperson how they derived their score and make a determination of what actions need to be taken. The sales manager can also evaluate and compare the entire pipeline of opportunities based on the Get score, the Go Score, and the Total Score (Get Score × Go Score ÷ 100).

More Accurate Forecasting

It's very common for sales professionals to exaggerate the probability of a deal, often based on the likelihood that a deal will eventually close. By closely monitoring both the Get Score and the Go Score, you add a strong dose of reality to the pipeline and often get a much more accurate representation of closing probabilities.

Consider a deal with a Get Score of 90. The buyer might be an existing client or a strong champion who is anxious to purchase. However, without a secure budget, the Go Score might only be around 30. This means the Total Score (Get x Go) is 27 (90 x 30 ÷ 100) or (in other words) the deal has a 27 percent probability of closing in the next ninety days. This is a harsh multiplier that may seem shockingly low to optimistic and eager sales professionals. But it also provides a terrific level of accuracy, especially to the sales management and executive teams, who rely upon accurate forecasts.

Works With Other Sales Methodologies

The concept of Get vs. Go is so simple, it can be introduced in just minutes and used anytime by any sales organization regardless of what tools, methodologies, or metrics a sales organization already has in place.

A sales manager may want to use Get vs. Go during their one-on-one meetings as they're walking through a salesperson's pipeline. Some sales organizations are very tied to their processes and methodologies and changing to an entirely new method or adjusting the CRM might be a bridge too far to cross. In such a case, Get vs. Go can be lightly implemented and layered on top of what they already have in place.

Meanwhile, our organization uses Get vs. Go to its fullest extent—it's at the heart of our sales process. We've integrated Get vs. Go into our CRM (which is generally easy to do with most mainstream CRM systems). When meeting one-on-one with my team, we analyze deals and discuss strategy through the lens of Get vs. Go. During larger meetings, with the CFO and CEO present, we'll discuss the entirety of our pipeline by referring to the Get vs. Go Total Score.

Think of Get vs. Go much like butter—you can lightly spread it on your dinner roll when desired, or you can choose to cook your entire steak in it (Ruth's Chris style). Regardless of how you use it, it can make your meal taste a little better.

Conclusion

At the beginning of this book, I shared a story from Singapore when I attended a conference and observed a business owner giving a sales presentation to a large group. I watched from a unique perspective as his presentation suffered and the audience lost attention. That experience led me down the path of researching content and curating my own material. The end result was my writing of this book.

Since that time, I've personally delivered hundreds of sales presentations. I've also heard many more presentations and listened to them with a heightened interest. Occasionally, I'm given the opportunity to speak at conferences. Somewhat recently, at a conference in Vancouver, British Columbia, Canada, I was given almost the exact same opportunity as that business owner in Singapore. At the beginning of the session, I had exactly five minutes to introduce myself and my company. So how did I do?

Using the concepts and frameworks that I've written about in this book, I crafted a five-minute pitch. I used the Opportunity + Solutions + Benefit framework (see chapter 4), and during the five minutes, I had just enough time for a couple of microstories (see chapter 6). I adhered closely to the concepts and guidelines from chapter 9 and practiced several times before my presentation.

The result? I received no standing ovation, nor did I expect one. What I did receive was attention and interest, as several people came up to me afterward and introduced themselves. Over the next couple of days, our booth had an influx of visitors who came by to chat and see our demonstration. At least one organization, who heard the presentation, made a significant purchase in the weeks following the conference.

Typically with most B2B sales, the results don't usually happen immediately. But over time, the successful efforts compound and the payoffs are significant.

Let me finish by sharing one final anecdote, combined with a small travel tip. Here it is . . .

Next time you're in France . . . try a hamburger.

I've had the good opportunity to visit France over a dozen of times in recent years, mostly on business, as I have an important client located in the Normandy region. There are many perks to visiting France, and at the top of the list is the French cuisine. The French are masters of the culinary arts, and there are some marvelous dishes to choose from: chicken confit, croque monsieur, and onion soup just to name a few.

Turns out the French have also mastered America's most famous culinary invention: the humble hamburger.

As a proud American and a hamburger connoisseur, it pains me to say it . . . but the French have turned the simple hamburger into an edible work of art that tastes even more delicious than it looks.

In France, the hamburger is considered more of a gourmet food than in America. When I'm in Paris, I like to visit a place called L' Artisan Burger. This restaurant specializes in hamburgers and literally employs acclaimed Michelin chefs to hand craft them. The price for a Parisian burger is gourmet as well . . . plan on at least €20. Totally worth it! Bon appétit.

In many ways a sales career is a bit like crafting a burger.

Technically, it doesn't take many qualifications. Just about anybody can flame broil a patty and toast some buns, just as anyone can slap together a proposal and deliver a half-baked presentation.

But when the stakes become high and there's serious money on the line, there's usually fierce competition. How good are your skills when there's a real cook-off?

Maybe you think your backyard burger is the best around, but then again, you could be competing against a Michelin-rated chef from France.

To become the best salesperson at your company, or even in your industry, you'll need to continue learning, practicing, and perfecting your craft. Cheers to those on a quest to become the best at whatever you are.

Notes

1   Brontén, George. "A Brief History of CRM: How We Got
    Here and What's Next." G2. August 22, 2022. https://learn.
    g2.com/history-of-crm.

2   Hodges, Jack. "CRM Statistics That Will Blow Your Mind."
    FiveCRM. May 17, 2023. https://www.fivecrm.com/blog/
    crm-statistics-that-will-blow-your-mind/.

3   Rhodes, Amber. "18 Buying Triggers for Identifying B2B
    Buying Cycles." Usergems. April 5, 2024. https://www.
    usergems.com/blog/buying-triggers.

4   Fs. "Ethos, Logos and Pathos: The Structure of a Great
    Speech." Fs. https://fs.blog/ethos-logos-pathos/.

5   Iannarino, Anthony. "The One Right Way to Talk
    About Your Competitor." Forbes. November 5, 2018.
    www.forbes.com/sites/forbesspeakers/2018/11/05/
    the-one-right-way-to-talk-about-your-competitor/.

6   "A Decade of Research Into How B2B Buyers Make Purchase
    Decisions." January 26, 2024. https://challengerinc.com/
    decade-research-how-b2b-buyers-make-purchase-decisions/

7   Aburumman, Nadine. "Nonverbal Communication in Virtual
    Reality: Nodding as a Social Signal in Virtual Interactions."
    ScienceDirect, Volume 164. August 2022. https://www.
    sciencedirect.com/science/article/pii/S1071581922000489#.

8   Cristiano, Brian. "5 Ways to Lose a Sales Pitch In the First
    5 Minutes." Bold.ceo. April 6, 2022. https://www.bold.ceo/
    business-growth/5-ways-to-lose-a-sales-pitch-in-the-first-5-
    minutes.

9   O'Connor, Casey. "Is BANT Still Effective in 2023? [Pros, Cons, Alternatives]." Yesware.com. May 31, 2023. https://www.yesware.com/blog/bant/.

10 Keenan. "Gap Selling: Getting the Customer to Yes: How Problem-Centric Selling Increases Sales by Changing Everything You Know About Relationships, Overcoming Objections, Closing and Price." 2019.

11 DeSantis, Dru. "The Dangerous Myth of the Rational B2B Buyer." DeSantis Breindel. September 16, 2023. https://www.desantisbreindel.com/insights/emotional-b2b-buyer"

12 "Backed Emotion in Business Marketing." 16, 2023. https://www.ana.net/miccontent/show/id/ii-2023-08-emotion-business-marketing#

13 Thomas, Julie. "Just Because Your Solution Is Different Doesn't Mean It Is Differentiated." Forbes. September 17, 2020. https://www.forbes.com/sites/forbesbusinessdevelopmentcouncil/2020/09/17/just-because-your-solution-is-different-doesnt-mean-it-is-differentiated/.

14 Gallo, Carmin. "The Art of Persuasion Hasn't Changed in 2,000 Years." Harvard Business Review. July 15, 2019. https://hbr.org/2019/07/the-art-of-persuasion-hasnt-changed-in-2000-years.

15 Clearsay Communications. "Presentations: Never Save the Best for Last." Clearsay Communications. September 30, 2019. https://www.clear-say.com/presentations-never-save-the-best-for-last/.

16 Pacini, Andrea. "Light vs Dark: What is the best colour for a slide background?" July 3, 2019. https://www.linkedin.com/pulse/light-vs-dark-what-best-colour-slide-background-andrea-pacini/

17 Gallo, Carmin. "A Long-Time Apple Designer Reveals Steve Jobs's 6-Step Rehearsal Process." Inc. October 8, 2018. https://www.inc.com/carmine-gallo/a-long-time-apple-designer-reveals-steve-jobs-6-step-rehearsal-process-he-used-for-every-presentation.html.

18 Van Edwards, Vanessa. "60 Hand Gestures You Should Be Using and Their Meaning.", Science of People. June 7, 2024. https://www.scienceofpeople.com/hand-gestures.

19 Lindner, Jannik. "Must-Know Public Speaking Statistics [Latest Report]." Gitnux. December 16, 2023. https://gitnux.org/public-speaking-statistics

20 Wortmann, Craig. "The Reality Check That May Save Your Company." Inc. February 13, 2014. https://www.inc.com/craig-wortmann/reality-check-could-save-your-company.html

Expanded Contents

Introduction 1
1 The Buyer's Journey 9
    Technology and Sales Organizations 11
    Unintended Consequences of Fancy CRMs 16
    The Buyer's Journey ARC 18
    Awareness Phase 20
    Research Phase 21
    Choice Phase 22
    Mapping the Buyer's Journey 23
2 Persuasion 27
    A Brief History of Persuasion 29
    Ethos, Logos, Pathos 30
    Powerful Examples of Ethos, Logos, Pathos 32
3 Sales Algebra 37
    The Best Strategy for the Awareness Phase 40
    The Best Strategy for the Research Phase 42
    The Best Strategy for the Choice Phase 44
    Order of Operations 45
4 Crafting a Sales Narrative 47
    Misdiagnosing a Prospective Buyer 49
    Steps to Crafting an Effective Sales Pitch 52
    What to Include in Your Presentation 53
        The Sports Car 54
        The SUV 55
        The Sedan 56
    Opportunity + Solution + Benefits Framework 57
        Introduce an Opportunity 58
        Present a Solution 58
        Share Benefits (Give an example) 59
    Selling to Someone With No Pain or Problems? . . . 60
    How to Differentiate 62

5 How to Build Credibility **65**
  The Reservoir of Credibility 67
    Company Credibility 68
    Personal Credibility 70
  Competence 71
    How to Increase Competence 71
  Reliability 72
    How to Increase Reliability 73
  Likability 73
    How to Increase Likability 76
      Conversational Ability 76
      Body Language: The Sunrise-Sunset Theory . . . 79
      Body Language as a Listener 80
      Winning Friends 82
  Authenticity 83
    The Original Sin of Selling 87
    Should You Withhold the Price? 88
    The Tension "Takeaway" Tactic 90
    Using the Right Tone 95
    Acting Too Excited and Talking Too Fast 98
  Confidence 99
    You Must Eat Your Own Dog Food 100
    Avoid Uptalk 101
  Credibility Is a Marathon 102
    Mining Old Leads 103
    The Power of a Sincere Mea Culpa 103
    Proactively Putting Yourself in the Spotlight 107
6 Microstories **109**
  How Retellable Is Your Sales Pitch? 111
  You Might Need Two Slide Decks 113
  Using Microstories 114
    The Microwave Anecdote 115
  Building a Catalog of Microstories and Anecdotes . 116
  Zooming In and Out 116
  Simple is Best 118

Memorize Your Material 119
The Conundrum with Discovery Questions 120
Asking Questions Is Like Dancing 122
Reciprocity in Conversation 125
What Are the Best Questions to Ask? 126
    BANT Questions 126
    GAP Questions 127
    Curiosity Questions 130
7 Emotional Selling 133
Do People Buy Based on Emotion? 135
What Stories Really Sell? 137
Sell Through the Eyes of the Love Group 138
The Power of Demonstration 140
The Battle of Gut Feeling 142
Longevity Leads to Bluebirds 143
8 Slide Deck Strategies 145
Define Your Objective 148
Identify Your Audience 148
Match the Method of Persuasion 148
Start Bold 149
How Will You Be Introduced? 150
3 High-Level Points 152
Use Opportunity + Solutions + Benefits 153
Strongest Points First 153
Build Your Leave-Behind Slide Deck 154
Connect Your Conclusion with Your Bold Start 154
Ask a Concluding Question 155
How to Polish Your Presentation 156
    Add Stories .156
    Add Questions 157
    Add Comedy 157
    Aesthetics 159
    Have Your Social Media Ready 159
9 Delivering Your Presentation 161
Practice Makes Perfect 163

Remove the Data. 165
Inspection Before Presentation 165
Body Language When Presenting. 166
Hand Gestures. .166
Too Loud Is Better than Too Soft 167
Remember to Slow Down 168
Eye Contact – Don't Look at the Display 169
Don't Apologize or Make Excuses. 169
It's Better to End Early. 171
10 Closing the Deal. 173
The Truth About Closing a Deal 175
ABC – Always Be Curious. 179
Sales Methodologies 180
11 The Get vs. Go Framework 183
How Does Get vs. Go Work? 185
Get vs. Go Examples 186
Scenario #1 186
Scenario #2 188
Scenario #3 190
Get Score Insights 192
The Best Strategy to Raise the Get Score? 192
Go Score Insights 194
The Best Strategy to Raise the Go Score 195
Advantages of Get vs. Go 196
Prioritize Opportunities 196
More Accurate Forecasting. 197
Works With Other Sales Methodologies. 198
Conclusion 201
Notes 205

Expanded Contents 209
Acknowledgements 215
About the Author. .217
Let's Connect. 219
Free Resources 221

Acknowledgements

Writing a book is an endeavor, and I'm thankful to my family for their continual support. The thanks and appreciation go well beyond the months of research and writing this book. There are sacrifices and life choices that go along with major career decisions. The constant travel and happenings of an international sales executive may seem exciting and glamorous at times, but there are some considerable downsides. I've missed my fair share of games, performances, and birthdays over the years, and I've missed milestones and emergencies when my family needed me nearby. However, the airline miles and travel benefits have been a nice perk—allowing us to make up for some lost time by traveling together on some amazing trips. (These are the moments and memories I treasure the most.) Special love to my children, Abby, David, Ben, Jacob, and Sarah. Most of all, love and thanks to my wife, Laura, who has shown incredible grit, strength, compassion, and determination in supporting me while raising children and progressing in her own career. Thank you also to my parents, David and LaVaun and my extended family for their continued support.

Also, special thanks to a few friends and colleagues who've provided encouragement, support, and advice over the years: Travis Isaacson, Ward Wilson, Kip Meacham, Eric Aroca, Jonathan McCurdy, Kolby Baron, and Monty & Karly Ball.

About the Author

When it comes to International Sales and Business Development, Brad has seen and done it all. Over the course of his career, Brad has been to every corner of the world selling technology and competing for multi-million-dollar projects. A B2B sales and marketing expert, he has delivered sales presentations (in-person) in over eighty countries and closed millions of dollars of business on six continents.

Brad is a Senior Partner and Vice President of Sales and Marketing at GlobalSim, Inc., a technology company that manufactures and sells high-end simulators throughout the world. He is also the founder of Blazer Sales and produces a variety of sales, training, and leadership material.

Brad holds an MBA from Brigham Young University and an executive certificate from the Kellogg School of Management at Northwestern University.

When not traveling, Brad enjoys boating and skiing with his family, along with hiking, pickleball, classic rock, and '80s music. Brad also enjoys creating and producing travel content on YouTube.

Let's Connect

Interested in learning more? Need a speaker or workshop trainer for your SKO or upcoming event? Reach out to Brad directly or follow him online:

brad@braddavidball.com

Linkedin.com/in/bradball

https://www.youtube.com/@blazersales

https://www.youtube.com/@bradball

Free Resources

A number of free resources are available to readers including charts, statistics, and other useful sales / marketing content.

www.braddavidball.com

www.ingramcontent.com/pod-product-compliance
Lightning Source LLC
Chambersburg PA
CBHW031847200326
41597CB00012B/312